ENGLAND'S RUIN

DISCUSSED

IN SIXTEEN LETTERS

TO

THE RIGHT HONOURABLE
JOSEPH CHAMBERLAIN, M.P.

BY

A. M. S. METHUEN

METHUEN & CO.
36 ESSEX STREET W.C.
LONDON

First Published in 1905

G

NOTE

FOR the facts contained in this book I am indebted to the ordinary treatises on political economy and to works on the more practical issues of the New Protection. From these I have not scrupled to borrow many valuable figures. I have derived the greatest assistance from Mr. Chamberlain's Free Trade Speeches, from various pamphlets issued by The Cobden Club, and (especially on the Imports and Exports) from Mr. L. G. C. Money's " Elements of the Fiscal Problem " —an admirable and lucid work. Mr. Money has been good enough to read my proofs and to check my figures. To the authors of other books I must express a general acknowledgment.

A. M. S. M.

February 8th, 1905.

CONTENTS

THE FIRST LETTER

OF CONDEMNATION TO DEATH

THE SECOND LETTER

OF A TIME LONG PAST

THE THIRD LETTER

OF THE NEW HISTORY

THE FOURTH LETTER

OF IMPORTS OF FOOD AND RAW MATERIALS

THE FIFTH LETTER

OF IMPORTS OF MANUFACTURES

THE SIXTH LETTER

OF EXPORTS

CONTENTS

THE TENTH LETTER

OF COUNTRIES LESS WISE

THE ELEVENTH LETTER

OF COLONIAL PREFERENCES

THE TWELFTH LETTER

OF RETALIATION

THE THIRTEENTH LETTER

OF A DRUNKEN HELOT

THE FOURTEENTH LETTER

OF FREE TRADE IN THEORY AND PRACTICE

THE FIFTEENTH LETTER

THE LAST LETTER

ENGLAND'S RUIN

THE FIRST LETTER

OF CONDEMNATION TO DEATH

SIR,—It is now nearly two years since the sober citizen, descending to his breakfast on May 16th, 1903, was astounded by the news of an impending cataclysm. He heard that his England was sick nigh unto death: the warning was on the wall, and the disease almost past the skill of the wisest surgeon. Nervous fingers unfolded the news sheet, and the appalling truth was made manifest. England is old; England is decaying; England must fall, unless strong arms embrace her. The enemy, cruel, malignant, with insidious and devilish arts, is at the gates. Unhappy citizen! he reads strange things and terrible. How our commerce is passing, our wealth but the shadow of a name, how Free Trade and the Little Englander have sapped our strength; how Protection is enlarging the girth and making strong the muscles of the Teuton and the Yankee. The Colonies are restless, their eyes are wandering to new lovers; and yet it is their help alone that can save the empire, their love must be retained at any cost and sacrifice. If the warning be unheeded and the surgeon uncalled—then England is doomed and the Empire in fragments.

Your desire was to rouse the British citizen from his complacent self-satisfaction, and you did not fail. All complacency indeed is sterile, and if your attack has shaken our sublime self-confidence without destroying our nerve, you are worthy of our thanks. But the speech at Birmingham was only the fusillade of blank cartridges. It was not until you turned your heavy guns on Mr. Cobden's statue that we knew we were in for real fighting.

Your attack you have developed with all the ardour and, may I say it, all the accuracy of your nature. North and South, East and West, you went forth, carrying wonder and dismay. We learnt that Free Trade was the most colossal fraud in the annals of history, that the picture of England in 1845 had been, in the interests of a Cobdenite tradition, grossly overpainted, that the poor of that date were, if not lapped in luxury, well-fed and contented, that the abolition of the Corn Laws was the work of a group of selfish manufacturers, intent on personal gain. We learnt that the prosperity of which we boast is but a phantom, that for the last thirty years our trade and wealth have been declining, that in place of amassing capital we have been heaping up a burden of debt to the foreigner, for our export trade is either declining or standing still, while our imports are growing at a merciless speed. You drew the dreadful conclusion that this excess of imports over exports was an " adverse balance "—a monstrous debt owing by us to our foreign creditors. You asked how long we could afford to spend more than we earned. You showed us how foreign nations were wounding or slaying our manufactures by the double process of preventing entry into their ports and of dumping their own goods on our impoverished land. The other nations, blessed by Protection, were advancing with the strides of giants. You compared the rapidly growing exports of Germany and America with our own stationary trade, of which you declared that the only healthy branch was our export trade to our own Colonies. Here, at last, you saw light : in the affection and support of our Colonies—to be bought at a price—you found the salvation of England. It was our duty to increase our trade with our Colonies, where a rapidly growing population, filled with patriotic zeal, would be willing not only to supply us with all the food which we require, but to buy from us the millions' worth of goods which they now buy from the foreigner. We must make an agreement with them : we must urge them not only to reduce or remove the duties which they place on British goods, but to promise never to manufacture articles which we now make and they do not make. Thus the Mother Country and her Colonies, interdependent, with no need of foreign commerce, the daughters feeding the mother and supplied by her with the things of art and industry, would come to form a mighty Empire—self-contained, self-sustained, and self-sufficing.   The opportunity was here and the accepted time : let it be embraced without delay, for the omens of portent and disaster were in every sky.

You pointed out that in order to induce the Colonies to cleave to us faithfully and to protect us, we must offer them something of value, and this something you found in a Preference to be granted to Colonial imports.   But as a Preference cannot be given unless there is something on which to give it, unless a corresponding tax be imposed, you proposed that duties should be laid on all imports, except raw materials, to be taken off in favour only of Colonial imports.   Your scheme was developed in each speech, and it ever held a fresh fascination for you.   For not only would it stay our Colonies from drifting from us, but it would renew our broken fortunes, rebuild our fallen industries, and make Britain a second Paradise.   No more would the foreigner lay his heavy duties on our goods.   To him we would thunder, " Two can play at your game.   Remove your duties, relax your duties.   If you will not, duties as high as yours shall burden your goods, not to be removed till yours shall go."   We should hold a pistol at his head ; and by Retaliation, a process most simple and most effective, force our rival to treat us with decency at last.

From this general exposition you proceeded to lay down a policy in detail.   On corn you would place a duty of 2s. a quarter, on flour a somewhat high tax to protect the miller.   On all meat (except bacon, the food of the very poor) you would impose 5 per cent., and on dairy produce a similar tax.   The consumer should feel no burden, for you hold that the seller pays the duty which the consumer escapes.   But in order to make assurance surer, you proposed to remit three-quarters of the tea tax, one half of the sugar duty, and part of the cocoa and coffee duties.   On manufactures you proposed to place duties not exceeding an average of 10 per cent. on the value ; while imports of Colonial manufactures would under your scheme of Preference enter free of all duty.   In the words of a great Englishman, you called in the New World to redress the balance of the Old.

Such was your diagnosis of our case, and such your cure.

Your attack on Free Trade produced a prodigious flutter: it made you more than ever the man of the moment, it seemed to make you the man of destiny. Men of business, bankers, merchants, manufacturers, shopkeepers, and a great host of respectable citizens, were vastly impressed by the new gospel spread before them. There was a prophetic strength in your denunciation, an amplitude and splendour in your outlook, which terrified and fascinated. Traders who imagined they were making £10,000 a year were cast into nervous dread lest their profits had been based on emptiness; manufacturers who had hitherto bartered their goods with the foreigner, receiving more than they gave, were filled with dim fears of adverse balances. At first it occurred to few that figures should be tested and compared; a savage and general gloom arose about us. But by degrees the unconquerable cheerfulness of the Englishman spread over us again, timidly, it is true, and with a proper sense of danger. Then Arithmetic and History began to lift up their heads, and our breath to come more steadily.

And can you marvel at the reaction? It is as though with dramatic suddenness a man were told in the prime of life and apparent health that his days are numbered, his heart unsound, his lungs destroyed. His neighbours are healthier, their hearts are sound as bells. Speedy death awaits him unless he takes the cure you thrust before him. The shock throws him into a panic fear—his imagination summons up the symptoms which you discover, and he is prostrate. The days pass, and life still remains; he begins to eat, to drink—most strange of all, he takes pleasure in his food, in his family, in the air of heaven. " Am I wasting away, and yet I see no outward signs? Is my heart diseased, and yet I feel no distress? " Prudence returns, and he does what he might have done before—he goes to his own doctor. He strips, and with pallid cheeks awaits the verdict. It soon comes. Joy of joys! he is as healthy as he was thirty years ago—no disease, no little sign of disease; a vigorous, sound, strong man. What! no organic trouble? no internal malady? Nothing. Here and here he ails—a little torpidity, a little over-indulgence; but at any serious trouble the doctor laughs aloud. But what of the sounder hearts of Jones and Smith: is not that a menace? A menace! Why? They are not more sound than yours, and are you to monopolize sound organs? For shame! Attend to your own business; live and let live. Brace up your energies, and leave quacks to doctor fools. You will be happier so. And so the man returns, sane and joyful, to his family and his daily work.

It was so with us. We began to question your figures and to doubt your history. We are, it is true, not as wealthy as we were in 1899, for we have been spending more than we earn. We are, perhaps, a little unintelligent, a little slow, a little lacking in ideas. But we feel vaguely that we cannot be as poor as you paint us; a balance is still at the bank, and we can sell all we make. Let us, before we take your medicine, see whether the disease has made the inroads which you describe.

Is our Empire falling in fragments? Are our sons across the seas so faithless that their love can only be bought by gold? Is it true? I see no proof of it, and, were it true, are we willing to hold our children with bonds so material? Is our trade passing from us? I take the tables of imports and exports, and I see a steady increase for half a century, and in these very years in which you proclaim our fall, I see greater figures than have gone before. Are our great industries decaying? You say so, and yet I see that each one grows apace in wealth and output. Is it a mirage? You say we are living on our capital, and yet I see the income-tax bringing a higher return each year, our oversea investments growing, our shipping growing. Have we been for many years heaping up debt by imports? If so, why does not the foreigner make us bankrupt? These things bewilder: vexatious though the quest may be, we must examine our ledgers, re-audit our balance-sheets, cast up again our accounts of profit and loss, read again our histories, and hear the other side. Pardon us if we do not at once accept your diagnosis and your remedy.

And now, sir, I ask your pardon and crave your patience. The letters which follow are not a treatise on political economy: they are the comment of a plain man on the practical issues of a policy. They deal with a problem which is both very complex and very simple, but into the deeper meanings and subtler shades I do not seek to penetrate. The simpler issues are enough for me and for my readers. I address these letters to you, because it is only through

your personality that I can hope to find the common man.
It is his fears and doubts that I seek to put to rest; his
weak knees, as he threads his embarrassed way through your
mazy garden, that I hope to strengthen. If on the way I
can reach your heart or your intelligence, I shall be proud
indeed; but it is not for you that I write. That would be
an act of impertinence and disproportion. The Man in the
Street is the object of my search, and are you not indeed his idol
and his type? Who moves him to such admiration? Who
can so fill him with the frenzy of patriotism? Your vigour,
your eloquence, your audacity, your hatred of the foreigner,
your very prejudices—all these are recognized by him as
his own. You are he; you make articulate his unutterable
and hazy thoughts; you are his Apotheosis. And it is not
without a touch of sympathy that I can speak to you—that is,
to him. Who has not felt, late or soon, seldom or often, what
you feel—your doubts, your distrust, your morbid fears, your
dread of the day when England shall be as Spain? The mood
comes to all. Let us see whether it is based on reality.

THE SECOND LETTER

SIR,—They say that some people can never see the things which surround them, but give them a fairy tale and all is clear. Let me, then, tell you a simple story. It is, I need not say, unfounded and impersonal. But it will serve.

Imagine a primitive nation of islanders, set in northern seas under a climate inhospitable but not unhealthy, and on a soil moderately fertile and rich. This people in its early years grew and dug all that was necessary for its sustenance; it neither visited nor was visited by other peoples: in a word it was self-sufficient. But the population increased, and with it came a scarcity of food and a certain restlessness, ambitious of adventure. Then boats were fashioned and entrusted to the seas. Bold men set forth and landed on a foreign shore. There they found strange foods and unknown luxuries. They asked of their new friends that they might carry these things to their own land, promising that they would in return bring them goods not seen in the stranger country. An agreement was made; the islanders were trusted and went back to their own people. They did a wondrous trade, and sold their imported goods to their countrymen for a high and profit-able price. Payment they received by barter in kind, and with a portion of the reward (retaining the rest as their own profit), they again set sail with their cargo and with some of the island merchants, and landed once more with their exports on the new shores. Again they were welcomed. The strangers received with delight the island goods, and besought the merchants to take back more of their products and to return with another shipload.

The commerce, thus begun, grew apace. Then the cumbrous method of exchange in kind was dropped and gold became the symbol of value, then coined money. But this, too, was found as cumbrous, and some ingenious man invented a method by which pieces of paper, sometimes called cheques and sometimes bills of exchange, were handed from one person to another as signs of value and honoured as though they were gold. New lands were discovered, with new foods, new treasures, new luxuries, until the island race with a great fleet of ships traded with all the world, bringing back every kind of thing necessary and luxurious, but always remembering to make a profit on its exchange. These profits, you must know, were very large, for besides the actual exchange of the goods, there were the great sums paid for the use of the ships (for the islanders had come to possess more than half the ships of the world). Also they had on their various voyages bought lands and houses in the foreign countries, and the rents of these lands were sent to the island and became an additional profit. Also the bankers who negotiated the cheques, and the insurance companies who insured the goods, and various other brokers and middlemen charged the foreigners for their services. All these sums were added to the profits of the islanders, and though they were not material goods, they had to be set down in the profit and loss account of the island race. And thus they were so fortunate that they made money on everything which they bought from foreign countries. No wonder that they became rich.

Now most of the other countries, being very jealous of the island, tried to keep out the goods of the islanders by placing heavy duties on the things which the island exported. The chief result of this was that the prices of everything in all foreign countries were much higher than they were in the island, and the workmen earned less wages and were fed on very poor food.

Then a strange thing occurred. Although the islanders were clearly growing wonderfully rich from their exchanges, and though the goods which they imported so cheaply were of great value and comfort to them, enabling them to live far more easily than of old, and actually giving hem many materials and things which could be produced

much better and more cheaply abroad than at home—
there were some grumblers. The islanders were a little
inclined to grumble. Some of the island manufacturers were
hurt by the goods which the other nations sent in, for as
these were imported at a low price, they could not sell their
own goods more dearly, and so they said, "Why should we
allow the accursed foreigner to send in things which we can
make just as well at home? Let us make him pay for importing them. Their merchants keep out foreign goods and
they make much money. Why should not we?" And they
chose as leader and spokesman a man with a very fluent tongue,
who advised the islanders to tax the foreigner. Unhappily
this advice was given when the people were suffering from
one of those periods of bad trade which always come to the
most prosperous, and as the leader had a loud voice and was
very commanding, the people listened to him. In an evil hour
they said, " We must protect our industries," and they put
small import duties on one or two things sent in, especially
on the goods manufactured by the grumblers. So these men
were satisfied : their goods were not undersold, and if
the import duty on the foreign thing was 5s., they were able
quickly to add 4s. to the price of their article, and to
make a large additional profit. Some people said this was
unfair on those who had before been able to buy it at 4s.
less ; but the merchants quickly silenced them, asking them if
they dared to question their personal honour, abusing the
foreigner, and calling their critics *Friends of every country but
their own.*

Now, if the rulers had stopped here and had not placed
import duties on anything else, the nation as a whole would
not have suffered very much ; but naturally the other manufacturers were not willing to see a few men pocketing all the
money ; and they, too, demanded Protection for their industries which were, they said, being ruined by the foreigner.
There was much opposition to this demand, because the wiser
men saw that if duties were put on everything, the rich
would have a monopoly and it would raise the price of every
necessity of life ; while the poor would have much trouble
in living at all. They also pointed out that the imports were
chiefly food and materials for making things cheaply to
use at home and to export abroad, and they said that if

they could not export cheaply they would lose half their export trade.

However, the jealousy of the foreigner was so great and the influence of the rich manufacturers so powerful, that they were able to bribe the rulers and to make them put duties on foreign goods. Of course, you must not suppose that the rulers actually took bribes in money, but the traders were very clever, and they knew how to bribe without seeming to bribe. For they would go to the relation of a ruler and tell him they would make him rich by good advice, and that perhaps if they did this he would plead for them with his cousin. And to each member of the Senate they sent petitions—each man asking that a duty should be placed on the thing which he himself made. And thus a Senator, even though he was a very good man, was not able to withstand the prayers of the merchants, especially when they told him that if he did not do what he was asked to do, he would suffer some inconvenience. These people then all said that the duties were very small, and they told the simple islanders that they would not have to pay more for the imports, because the foreigners would very kindly pay the duties themselves, and the islanders would buy things at the same price as before. But these very cunning merchants had made up their minds that if they could keep out the foreign goods, they would be able to raise the price of their own goods also and to make much money. They also had bought many newspapers, and these papers, being the property of the greedy manufacturers, were obliged to say what they were told to say, and they nearly all advised Protection, and said it was a very patriotic thing to keep out foreign goods. You would scarcely believe what foolish things these men said. They seemed to think that any statement was good enough for the people. Thus they said it was a very bad thing to receive things from abroad and to sell them in the island or to send them abroad at a profit, because this signified that the island lost on the business. Up to that time people had thought just the opposite.

Now there were many islanders who were really very fond of their own country and wanted to help it, and did not want to make any profit out of their fondness, and so the men who did want to make profits persuaded these honest men to help them, and they themselves were able to look very honest and respectable in their company. And men said, "These must be very noble Patriots." And so these men got up very solemnly and without smiling, and told the people that they would be much happier and richer if they kept out foreign goods and only bought things made in the island. Therefore the greedy manufacturers said very often and all together, that it was out of pure love of their country that they advised Protection, but really they cared less about their country than they did about their profits, and only wanted to raise the price of everything which they sold. This they called sometimes Patriotism and sometimes the Imperial Spirit. People had such curious names for things in those days.

All these men were very rich, and rich people, who don't mind what they say, can easily persuade others. For few people examine what they are told, and if you say a thing three times and very loudly, they will believe you. So at last it was decided to place import duties on everything, and the result was extraordinary and really terrible. You would have thought that in any case only the goods imported from abroad would have increased in price by the amount of the duty. But, as a matter of fact, the island manufacturers put up the price of nearly everything they sold. For instance, the landlords had forced the rulers to tax foreign wheat heavily, so that they might get more for their wheat. The loaf, therefore, which before cost only 4d., rose to 7d. and 8d., and the Patriots said this was really good for the people, because it was nobler to eat dear island bread than cheap foreign bread. Some people took a long time to understand this. Meat, too, rose greatly in price, and the poor had to give up meat. Some of them grumbled, but the rulers said that not to eat meat was very Imperial, because the simpler life was better for the country, and meat often brought disease. And clothes also were very dear, and timber, and paper, and the things which you buy at grocers, like mustard and salt and jam, were all half as dear again as they used to be. This, the loud-voiced man said, was an excellent thing, for the people had before worshipped a false deity—the Demon of Cheapness—and now they could praise the True God—the God of Dearness.

And so the great orator and his followers were very happy,

and the imports from the foreigner were greatly reduced, and the island exports were for a time greater than the imports. This seemed a glorious victory, but soon the exports grew very small also. For, as you know (but the loud-voiced man doubted this), trade with other countries is done by exchange of goods, and if people do not import things from abroad they cannot very well export things to pay for them. The islanders, too, found their trade with foreign countries only half what it was, because the foreigner now said he could buy more cheaply at home. And thus the trade both into and out of the island grew less and less. Finally, owing to the great increase in the cost of living and of materials, the things manufactured were sold so high that only half the former numbers were bought at home. Another thing naturally followed. The export and import trades being reduced by one-half, only half the number of ships were wanted, and not only were no new ships built, but the others were broken up or sold to the foreigners, who began to increase their own business at the expense of the island race. The worst of all was that trade became so bad that thousands of workmen were thrown out of work, and as all food had gone up greatly in price, there were crowds of starving men and women and children, and the scenes all over the island were heart-breaking.

Then the people began to see how they had been deceived, and to clamour for Freedom of Trade and the removal of all those duties which were intended to make prices high. But, as you imagine, many of the manufacturers, although some were suffering very much, were making much money, and they said (what was quite true) that to alter the financial (or, as they called it, the fiscal) arrangements would throw everything into confusion, and the rulers and the newspapers repeated what they said. They said also they were very sorry for the unemployed, and the only thing for them was to eat less.

But soon the harvest failed, and there was a great famine and a terrible revolution, and the loud-voiced man had to fly from the country, and some of his fellow-conspirators were caught by the mob and hanged in a square in the chief city, near the monument of a great sailor—they, the curse of their land, under the image of the man whoᵥ₄d once saved his nation. And though this was a somewhat forᵣible thing to do, most people felt that, as the acts of these meᵤ had caused the misery and death of so many, they had met with their deserts. And then the rulers were cast out and new ones were appointed, and trade was made quite· free again. And happiness and prosperity returned to the island.

THE THIRD LETTER

SIR,—You have doubtless noticed that the easiest way to secure an audience is to be bold in paradox. Thus to assert that black is white, that virtue is vicious, that Napoleon never lived, that Nero was a lamb, is to win a hearing and a name. It is, I imagine, with this harmless ambition that you have deserted the domains of arithmetic for the more dignified fields of history. The same methods are visible. You make up your facts and your figures as you go along, and the results are delightful and unconventional. Thus you tickle your hearers with this new reading :—

"Is it true that at the time when Free Trade was introduced, and the Corn Laws were repealed, we were in a state of destitution and misery and starvation? Is it true that under the Protection which prevailed before that this country was going down in the scale of nations, or losing its prosperity and losing its trade? No, absolutely no. The exact reverse was the case."

I am aware that this is only a rhetorical pleasantry, but Protectionists have short memories, and for them and for others let me in a few pages give a picture of those halcyon days.

The story is soon told. In the Forties, after a succession of bad harvests, the mass of the people were starving : they did not live, they existed. The long war with France had raised the price of wheat to an enormous figure, and the landowners' chief ambition was by keeping up the war prices to establish a monopoly and to avoid a reduction in their rents. The privileges of the landowner had been elevated into a sacred right, bound up with the well-being and very existence of the

State. The fallacy of the Protectionist has always been to divide one interest from another, to separate the privileges of the land from the rights and necessities of other interests, and their dogma was that the community must suffer that the landlords alone may wax fat. After corn, sugar was the special care of the legislature. Sugar and corn have always been near the heart of the aristocrat, and it is on these two necessities of life that the tariff-monger delights to lay his hands. Law after law was passed against the importation of foreign corn, and the agitation against the Corn Laws was a struggle against dear bread. In 1773 the importation of foreign wheat was forbidden as long as English wheat was not more than 48s. per quarter. In 1791 a duty of 24s. 3d. was imposed as long as English wheat was less than 50s. a quarter; if English wheat was over 50s., the duty was 2s. 6d. In 1804 foreign corn was practically prohibited from importation if English wheat was less than 63s. a quarter; in 1815 the prohibition was extended till the price of English wheat was 80s. a quarter. The same policy was extended to all imports, until in 1846 no less than 813 articles were taxed to protect the industries of Great Britain. Preferences, too, were given to Colonial imports with little advantage to any one. As you may easily conclude, the duties were so vexatious that they strangled our trade, and so onerous that by reducing imports they failed to benefit the Treasury. The country was half ruined in order to add to the revenue half a million a year. But some one must have gained, you will say. Yes, some one did gain. The protected industries made three pounds for every pound that the State gained. And who paid the whole? The unhappy consumers, of whom the poor bore a share wickedly and immeasurably greater than the rich. This damnable greed and folly produced its inevitable results. In 1842

" the whole of the labourers in the agricultural districts were on the verge of starvation. The poor rates were in some districts 20s. in the pound. At the time of which I am speaking the large towns were described by eye-witnesses as bearing the appearance of beleaguered cities, so dreadful was the destitution and the misery which prevailed in them. People walked the streets like gaunt shadows, and not like human beings. There were bread riots in every town.

There were rick-burnings on all the country sides. We were on the verge of a revolution when the Corn Laws were abolished."

" I think it inconceivable that the working classes of this country will ever again submit to the sufferings and to the miseries which were inflicted upon them by the Corn Laws in order to keep up the rents of landlords. If that is the programme of the Tory party we have only in answer to it to recall the history of those times when Protection starved the poor, and when the country was brought by it to the brink of revolution. Remember the description which was given in the verses of the Corn Law Rhymer of the sufferings endured by the people and of the burning indignation the sufferings called forth :—

> " ' They taxed your corn, they fettered trade,
> And every good that God hath made
> They turn to bane and mockery.
> They knew no interest but their own,
> They shook the State, they shook the throne,
> Oh, years of crime ! ' . . . .

That is not a retrospect which I think would be favourable to any party or any statesmen who should have the audacity to propose that we should go back to those times."

These are strong words. Whose words are they ? They are from two speeches by Mr. Chamberlain in 1885, and they are true. Read what Macaulay said in 1845 :—

" Will anybody tell me that the capitalist was the only sufferer, or the chief sufferer ? Have we forgotten what was the condition of the working people in that unhappy year ? So visible was the misery of the manufacturing towns that a man of sensibility could hardly bear to pass through them. Everywhere he found filth and nakedness, and plaintive voices, and wasted forms and haggard faces. Politicians, who had never been thought alarmists, began to tremble for the very foundations of Society. First the mills were put on short time. Then they ceased to work at all. Then went to pledge the scanty property of the artisan ; first his luxuries, then his comforts, then his necessaries. The hovels were stripped till they were as bare as the wigwam of the Dogribbed Indian. Alone amid the general misery, the shop with the three golden balls prospered, and was crammed from cellar to garret with the clocks and the kettles, and the blankets, and the Bibles of the poor. I remember well the effect which was produced in London by the unwonted sight of the huge pieces of cannon which were going northward to overawe the starving population of Lancashire."

. . . .

" If these things do not teach us wisdom we are past all teaching. Twice in ten years we have seen the price of corn go up, and as it went up the wages of the labouring classes went down. Twice in the same period we have seen the price of corn go down, and as it went down the wages of the labouring classes went up. Surely such experiments as these would in any science be considered as decisive."

The foreign trade was scanty and depressed. The rulers of the State held the views to which you are subservient, and their touchstone of policy was the prohibition of imports. They could not be made to see that if foreign imports are forbidden, exports, for which alone imports can be exchanged, are also stopped. By checking the importation of corn they were therefore reducing the British export trade to miserable proportions.

The whole country, indeed, was on the edge of bankruptcy. Great firms collapsed, workmen in tens of thousands were dismissed; the farmers, half ruined by the excessive fluctuations of corn prices, were in almost as evil a plight as their labourers, to whom bread was a luxury, and turnips and potatoes a staple food. In the country districts wages were 8s. a week with hours as long as the master chose to decide. The 4-lb. loaf was 1s., tea could be bought at 8s. a pound, and bad sugar at 8½d. " Crammings " were a welcome variation on swedes, and barley cake was a boon. Do not speak of village idylls when a Somerset labourer had to frame such a budget as this :—

			s.	d.					s.	d.
Wages...	...	...	7	0	Rent ...	...	...	1	0
					½ bushel of wheat	...	4	0
					Grinding, baking, &c.	0	6
					Firing ...	...	...	0	6
					Balance	...	...	0	6
								7	0

The balance of sixpence was for the clothes, potatoes, and miscellaneous expenses of himself and his family. The bread-tax extorted from the labourer and artisan *one-fifth* of his whole income, while from the nobleman it took one halfpenny in every hundred pounds. No wonder that the people died off in droves.

In the towns things were no better. In 1841 there were 2,000 houses empty in Preston, and in Leeds there were 20,000 people whose average earnings were under a shilling a week. In Manchester, 12,000 families had pawned all their furniture and nearly all their clothing. As the wages sank so did the food rise and the hours of work increase. Every kind of crime was rampant. Arson, rick-burning, sheep-stealing, bread riots, poaching, smuggling, were inevitable. Never in the history of our country has so piteous a time been recorded.

Do you imagine that the country was being spoilt by prosperity when the Queen was obliged to use these words to Parliament in 1842 ?—

" I have considered with deep regret the continued distress in the manufacturing districts of the country. The sufferings and privations which have resulted from it have been borne with exemplary patience and fortitude."

Again, you say that before 1846 we had secured a supremacy of the world's markets, and that our prosperity after that date had nothing to do with Free Trade. I will put two disproofs against this. One is a quotation from a petition to Parliament of the Manchester Chamber of Commerce in 1838 :—

" Your petitioners view, with great alarm, the rapid extension of foreign manufactures, and they have, in particular, to deplore the consequent diminution of a profitable trade with the Continent of Europe. . . . Whilst the demand for all those articles in which the greatest amount of the labour of our artisans is comprised, has been constantly diminishing, the exportation of raw material has been as rapidly increasing."

The other is a table showing the average value of our exports from 1831 to 1864. I ask you to compare the figures before and after 1846.

AVERAGE VALUE OF EXPORTS OF BRITISH PRODUCE AND MANUFACTURES.

				£
1831-35	...	...	...	...	40,500,000
1836-42	...	...	...	...	50,011,000
1843-48	...	...	...	...	56,742,000
1849-53	...	...	...	...	75,245,000
1857-59	...	...	...	...	98,900,000
1860-64	...	...	...	...	132,400,000

But with the necessity came the man. The manufacturers, at first Protectionists to the core, were bewailing no exports and a poor home market for their wares, and they were therefore in the humour to listen to the words of a noble Englishman. Richard Cobden, the object of your modern shafts, was a man of marvellous energy, of clear honesty and of supreme common sense. For seven years he worked ceaselessly with Villiers and Bright against the prejudices and interests of the aristocracy.

The success of the Anti-Corn Law League was slow in coming. The Protectionists were well entrenched and copiously supplied with the articles of their creed. *The price of corn was the test of national prosperity. The poor were not meant to be well fed. The aristocracy was the chief support of the nation, and their incomes must be maintained. The Corn Laws were established to secure plenty. Better the breezy call of incense-breathing morn, and the neat cottage, than the sad sound of the factory bell.* Lord George Bentinck used an argument with which you are not unfamiliar :—*The working classes would be better off with undiminished wages and wheat at 70s. per quarter than with corn at 45s. and reduced means of procuring it.* The Ministers of the Established Church, forgetting, as they have too often forgotten, that no one had denounced the greed of the rich or had defended the cause of the poor with greater passion than the Founder of their religion, presented a solid front against the reformers. A dean told the poor that if they had no bread there were plenty of mangel-wurzel. The Duke of Norfolk placed a further refinement on this exquisite jibe and recommended curry-powder.

But facts were beginning to find their way to the fears or to the intelligence of the rulers, and to the conscience of the nation. By slow degrees the approaches to the fortress were carried, and in 1845 the fortress was stormed. The failure of the potato crop in Ireland was as it were an act of God, and no one could resist His hand. The Corn Laws were repealed by a majority of 98 on May 15th, 1846.

You are bold enough to tell your hearers that dear bread was not the cause of the repeal of the Corn Laws, and that this repeal did not produce at once a reduction in the price of bread. Surely of all your assertions this is one of the most extraordinary. The piteous facts I have put before you dispose of your first audacity; your second is disproved by this table:—

PRICES OF WHEAT PER QUARTER.

			s.	d.				s.	d.
1844	...	...	51	3	1849	...	...	44	3
1845	...	...	50	10	1850	...	...	40	3
1846	...	...	54	8	1851	...	...	38	6
1847	...	...	69	9	1852	...	...	40	9
1848	...	...	50	6	1853	...	...	53	3
	Average	...	55	5		Average	...	43	5

Remember that though the Corn Laws were repealed in 1846, the duties were not at once abolished, but remained until 1849. If you point to 1854-6 as years of dear bread, should you not also tell your audience that they were the years of the Crimean War, when Russian supplies were stopped, and wheat rose to 72s.?

The repeal of the Corn Laws was the knell of Protection. By sure and steady steps Protective duties were abolished, and in 1869 scarce a vestige of the tariff remained. The remission of the duties had been opposed by the Protectionists with rage and fury. They pictured a navy and a mercantile marine ruined, British industries abolished, and the whole land flooded with our rivals' wares. The Free Traders were accused of a desire to discharge all British labourers, and to employ foreign workmen in their place. The *Times* exhausted its vocabulary of elegancies. Mr. Cobden was a capering mercenary, the author of incendiary clap-trap. Other respectable papers showed equal insight. The League was a foul combination, and its chiefs ignorant demagogues, bloodsuckers, assassins in will if not in act.

The results of the abolition of the Corn Laws and the gradual freeing of trade are too striking to need more than a summary. When you find that after this measure our export and import trades rose at once and greatly, that we began to import more gold than we exported, that our merchant fleet doubled in ten years, that the National Debt was steadily diminished, that the aggregate wealth of the nation began to grow enormously, that the savings of the poor began to exist, and emigration to decrease, that crime and pauperism diminished by one-half, that wages rose and food became cheap—what more need we say?

Here, then, is the justification of this simple and noble experiment, and here is the answer to your sneers. In all classes a higher standard of comfort is given by a fall in the price of all commodities, and the free and unfettered exchange of commerce. Fifty years which show an enormous increase of wealth among the whole population, a growing return from the income-tax, a growing balance at the bank, larger investments at home and abroad—this half century is eloquent of the blessings which you deny. For the poor the boon has been the greatest. Cheap and generous food instead of starvation, good wages instead of a poor pittance, regular employment instead of infrequent work,* the power of saving instead of debt, honest work and innocence where pauperism and crime had filled the workhouses and gaols.

The past recedes from our sight and the prosperity of 1905 may dim the realities of 1842. You say dear bread can never come again. But does not dear wheat make dear bread, and are not landlords as human now as they were sixty years ago?

---

* The increase in our population has led to no decrease in employment. On the contrary—put on one side the temporary depression due to the South African War—employment is more constant and wages higher. In cash wages it is reckoned that if a man earns to-day 25*s.* he would have been earning 13*s.* 9*d.* in 1840 with food *nearly twice as dear.* Not only have cash wages risen, but by the fall in the price of food real wages, i.e. that which a man obtains in exchange for his money, have risen. What a man can now buy for 9*s.* he could have bought for not less than 16*s.* in 1840.

B

THE FOURTH LETTER

SIR,—It is clear that all imports are hateful to you, that if you had your will, nothing made or grown in a foreign land should enter a British port. You would wish us to feed only on British meat and corn, to drink British wines out of British glasses, to smoke British cigars, to wear British silk, to admire ourselves in British mirrors. Cheapness is to you an abomination : competition the incarnation of evil. Let us live on simple English fare—and pay dearly for it. Let us use only things manufactured by our own artificers—and make our country richer by giving twice as much for them. This is your simple creed. It was also the creed of Lord George Bentinck, as it was probably the creed of the men of the stone age. But we abandoned it sixty years ago. Our forefathers, in the exercise of their wisdom or unwisdom, determined that this self-containment was impossible or impolitic, and British merchants and sailors were allowed to bring imports from foreign lands without prohibitive taxes, and to take in return and payment British goods to the alien countries. Let us now see whether this policy was so ruinous as you would have us to believe ; let us even see whether the free importation of food and the necessaries of life, of raw material, and of semi-raw materials for our manufactures, is not necessary to our existence as a great commercial nation.

It is clear that you do not propose at present to forbid the importation of foreign food, or to place a very high duty on it. You are therefore in agreement with us that such foreign imports are in our present imperfect state of civilization necessary, though gradually to be discouraged in favour of home-grown food and Colonial produce. You will see, if you refer to the analysis of our food imports in the Board of Trade Report, that we import over £200,000,000 a year of food, which has been well called the raw material of human beings. We import £48,000,000 of meat, £70,000,000 of grain and flour, £21,000,000 of butter, £6,000,000 of eggs, and nearly £6,000,000 of cheese. Of these vast and necessary supplies the Colonies send us only about *one-fifth*. We import sugar to the value of £18,000,000, and of this, even under your Sugar Convention, only £700,000 is Colonial sugar. Tea comes chiefly from our Colonies. Of barley, oats, and maize we import to a great extent, and practically all comes from the foreigner. Add other food supplies, which it would be tedious to give in detail, and you see a grand total of £215,000,000. Does not this vast amount of provisions, without which our teeming population would starve, force upon us three questions?

1. Could we grow either here or in our Colonies sufficient food to replace the supplies which the foreigner sends us?

2. Would British and Colonial supplies be as unfailing and secure, and ought we to endanger our foreign supplies and their cheapness by any act of commercial hostility?

3. What effect will the reduction of our imports have upon our export trade?

These are vital questions, and they demand a sincere consideration. How will you answer the first question? You will not assert that we can grow enough corn at home for our population, and the simplest can see that even if we do grow more corn, we must depend chiefly on oversea supplies. If you answer, "*I do not ask the British farmer to grow more wheat; I shall summon that from our Colonies across the seas,*" I wish to know how the British farmer will be benefited if wheat comes in free from the Colonies in place of free wheat from the foreigner? Will not the farmer tell you that your promise of a new prosperity for agriculture is a false dream if British prices are kept down by Colonial corn, and will you be able to refuse his demand for Protection against Colonial imports? If you grant it and place a duty on Colonial corn, you destroy your Colonial preference, and your own theory proves that your action will carry the disruption of the Empire.

The second point is of almost equal difficulty. It is absolutely necessary that we should have the whole world as our food market. The capacity of each country varies from year to year, and we can depend neither on the foreigner nor on the colonial for a steady and equable supply. Now the harvest in America is poor and her supply diminishes, but India comes to the rescue ; now Australia fails, but America sends us enough and to spare. The importance of the foreign supply has yet another aspect. Imagine a war with a European power, and the Colonies alone supplying us with food. The ships importing Colonial (i.e. British) corn, at the mercy of any cruiser or privateer, will pass through countless risks to reach our harbours with cargoes enhanced by those very risks to famine prices. But let our supplies come from America and Russia also, and our enemy will not dare to fire a shot against the argosies of Russia and the great Republic. Are you serious in your ambition that we should alienate the nations which feed our people on the chance that one of our Colonies may be able, after the lapse of many years, to grow enough corn to feed us ? By all means persuade our Colonists to grow more wheat and to rear more cattle and sheep. This they will do without our encouragement, but how long will it be before they reach the height of our necessities, and how do you propose that we shall live in the interval ?

Your answer to the third question must be that to reduce our imports is to reduce our exports. You understand the theory of exchange, and you know that we pay for our imports by our exports : we do not pay by gold. If then you lessen the volume of our imports, whether of food or of manufactures, you are by this very act depriving the foreigner of his ability to buy our manufactures, and you are robbing our manufacturers of a market for their wares.

Let us now examine your programme in detail and test it by figures. You propose to place a duty on all corn (except maize) imported from foreign countries, and from this duty you may be able to raise a revenue of three or four millions for the Exchequer,* less the expenses of collection. But see

* I take this estimate from Mr. Money's book. He bases it on the figures of 1902, and his calculations should be studied in detail.

the ill-favoured thing which follows. All prices tend to the same level, and if you raise foreign goods to a given price, the home-made and the Colonial article will be sold at or just under that price. Never forget that the object of a protective duty is to raise the price of a thing ; otherwise it has no meaning, and the "ruined" industry will be as ruined as before. Now our foreign supplies of corn form only a fraction of our whole consumption, and the cost of this consumption will rise almost to the amount of your duty. Assuming that no less foreign corn is imported and that the consumption of home and Colonial corn remains the same, the British consumer will, by the extra price he has to pay, be robbed of double the amount that goes into the Treasury. Surely this is clear. You put a duty of 6*d.* on a foreign import. What was sold before at 2*s.* is therefore now sold at 2*s.* 6*d.*, *but the home-made thing also rises to 2s. 6d.*, only the 6*d.* on the foreign article goes into the Exchequer, while the consumer has to pay the extra 6*d.* not only on the foreign thing, but on the home and colonial article as well, the rise on which goes not to the Treasury but to the producer. A similar result from a similar rise in price will follow your 5 per cent. duties on meat and dairy produce. By your whole food taxes you benefit the Treasury by £5,000,000, and the Colonists by £1,500,000, while you take out of the pockets of the British consumer at least £15,000,000. Of these millions about *one-third* will go into the Treasury, while the other two-thirds pass into the pockets of the landowners and the Colonists.

You say you will refund any loss by reducing the taxes on tea and sugar, but as these are war taxes and should be reduced in any case, the consumer will probably be less grateful than you expect. And if you reduce these duties the Treasury will gain less than ever.

This seems a very admirable way of filling the Exchequer. And do not forget this—that the higher duty you impose, the less food will be imported and bought, and the less duty will be paid into the Treasury. The more you tax, the less will your taxes bring you.

Another thing is equally certain. Your duties will be modest at first, but if they are to benefit the Colonies and to protect our own industries they will and they must be increased. A small duty is not protective, and if you will glance at the official figures, you will see how, sometimes slowly, sometimes at a leap, the landlords and farmers of Germany have forced the Government to raise the duties on imported wheat from 1s. 2d. a quarter to 11s. Do you think that our landlords and farmers will be content with a 2s. duty on corn? No less a duty than 10s. will protect them, and 10s. they will get if your policy is triumphant.

Do not think that the foreigner will pay the whole duty. It may be laid down as an axiom that an import duty on a single article which is not of necessity must generally raise the price of that article. It need not raise it by the whole amount of the duty, because the demand slackens. If, however, the article is necessary to human life, the demand cannot greatly slacken, and the consumer not only pays the chief part of the duty, but he may pay something more. He may pay for the cost of collection and his share of the increased price of everything resulting from the higher cost of living to the whole population. The producer—whether British or foreign—raises his price, and the foreigner does not pay more than a fraction of the duty himself. You say, in defiance of all reason and experience, that the foreigner will pay the duty, and that the consumer will pay no more than before. If you believe that, why do you except bacon from duty because it is the food of the poorest? Why do you except maize? If you still doubt, pray look at the prices of wheat in France and England from 1890 to 1897—the years in which France was obliged, owing to a shortage in the harvest, to import wheat.

	French Price.		English Price.		French excess over English Price.		French Duty.	
	s.	d.	s.	d.	s.	d.	s.	d.
1890 ...	44	1	31	11	12	2	8	9
1891 ...	47	10	37	0	10	10	8	9
1892 ...	41	6	30	3	11	3	8	9
1893 ...	37	9	26	4	11	5	8	9
1894 ...	34	6	22	10	11	8	8	9
1897 ...	43	9	30	2	13	7	12	2

Here you will see that not only did the Frenchman pay the whole of the duty levied on corn, but that he paid in every year more than the duty in addition to the normal price of wheat. You will find also in the Blue Book that in 1903 in France, Germany, and Italy, the people were paying the price of wheat *plus* the duty *plus* an additional sum. This is the fatal and inevitable law :—First a trifling copper, then silver it becomes, then a golden tax—paid with compound interest by the poorest in the land.

See another result. The death rate falls with cheap wheat and rises with dear wheat. Crime, pauperism, and vagrancy increase with the growth of taxes and the rising price of food. The war taxes of 1900–1904 have increased the price of food by at least £20,000,000 a year, an increase which falls far more heavily on the masses with their small incomes than on the richer classes with their large margins. Crime and pauperism have grown ; how monstrous will they be when you have your will.

Here, then, is the root of the matter. We import into these islands every year a vast amount of the best food in the world, bought at the lowest prices, in order that our people, well fed and nourished, may be able to sustain the struggle of existence. Of this food not less than four-fifths comes from foreign countries. How shall we strike at these countries by Retaliation, Protection, or Preference, without endangering the sustenance of our people, their strength, and their very life?

And now, having dealt with the raw materials of life and discovered that you wish us to tax four-fifths of the food which we import, let us look into our imported supplies of the things which are necessary for the manufacture of British goods. And first you must notice that not only are absolutely raw and semi-raw or crude materials necessary, but that what is imported as a completely manufactured article becomes on its arrival here a basis of an article of greater finish and perfection. Not only do we require such raw materials as indiarubber, cotton, wool, flax, and hemp, marble, wood for paper, and timber for building, and such crude or half-manufactured things as cotton, woollen and linen yarns, unwrought copper, oils and tallow, but our manufacturers would be hard pressed without the host of finished things which are the very tools of their labour. It would divert capital and labour from more profitable industries if we had to make all the boiler-plates, the glass, the wood-ware, the machinery, the paper, the paint, and the thousand other things which the foreign manufacturer contributes at a low rate to the raising of the great edifice of our prosperity.

On raw materials, and perhaps on crude materials, you do not at present propose to lay a tax, but how long will they escape your paternal care? And let me tell you in all seriousness that a twofold necessity will force you to impose a tax on raw imports. In the first place, Colonial Preference is in the forefront of your scheme. Can you, then, deny the claim of South Africa to a Preference on wool, of Australia to a Preference on wool, of Canada to a Preference on timber? If the Empire can only be held together by Preferences, then each Colony must see that its own products come into Britain on more advantageous terms than those imposed on the foreigner.

Secondly, the weapon of Retaliation, dear to Mr. Balfour and Lord Lansdowne, will and can only be used against America and Russia in the form of a duty on their cotton, corn, tallow, and hemp. We are, then, without doubt committed at once or in the future to import duties on practically all our raw materials. Have you ever considered what this means to British trade? Of cotton we import vast quantities from America and a trifling amount from the Colonies. Will you then tax one of the greatest industries of Britain for the sake of a paltry gain to a few Colonials; will you dislocate and throw into permanent confusion and unrest the whole of Lancashire; will you imperil this gigantic home and export trade? But you say, and doubtless in all sincerity, "*I am opposed to duties on raw materials and on cotton most of all!*" I answer that as a Protectionist you are no longer master of yourself. You are opposed to nothing except to the foreigner: your one object is to keep down foreign imports—that is your whole *raison d'être*. You must follow whither your demon leads you. If you are to prefer Colonial cotton, if you wish to retaliate on America for her duties on our manufactures, you must retaliate on her cotton and her corn.

You wish, perhaps, to encourage the Colonies to send us iron. Nothing easier: you place a 5 per cent. duty (quite a little duty, you say) on foreign iron, and let the Colonial iron in free. It is an old remedy tried by us in former years: all your remedies are old—as old as human folly. But the duty is not availing, and the foreign iron still arrives. You increase your duty to 10 per cent. or 12½ per cent. What is the result? You say that the foreigner will pay the duty.

But you are wrong. The British importer and ultimately the British consumer will pay it. Are you sceptical? Then let me place before you an interesting document, the estimate of English iron imported into Spain. I quote it from a newspaper :—

	£	s.	d.
Ironwork f.o.b. per ton	8	17	6
Freight to Bilbao	0	11	0
Import-duty, or *Protection*	5	15	0
Handling, railway freight, and other charges	1	7	6
Per ton, delivered in Madrid ...	£16	11	0

What does the Spanish manufacturer do? Spain is rich in iron and he could supply the ironwork at the English price, £8 17s. 6d. But he is "protected" from competition, and he charges his customer £16 8s. 6d. That is, he puts practically the whole of the duty into his own pocket.

So will it be under your tariff. *All* iron, home and foreign, rises in price. The ship-building, the hardware, the ironmongery and allied trades, see their expenses raised by at least 15 per cent., their tenders are raised by that amount or more, and every article rises in price. Ships, hardware, tools, joists, and bolts, nails, screws, all soar on ambitious wings to the Protectionist heaven of high prices. Rents are raised in house and cottage all over the kingdom, ships and factories cost 20 per cent. more than before, the expenses of manufacture are increased in proportion, less workmen are employed, and the end is stagnation and depression. Who shall estimate the enormous loss which you will lay upon us with your blind revenges on the nations which supply us with our food and strength? And allow that in a few years (as you assert) the Colonies can supply us with all we need—will our iron-masters be content to see Colonial iron dumped down on England's shores where foreign iron had come before? Will they not cry aloud for Protection against the children who are strangling their Mother's industries?

Again, you are urged to keep out hides, stone, manures, tallows, oils, yarns, and lead. You are told that these things can be produced in Britain by trades now half ruined by foreign competition. A word is enough: a duty of $7\frac{1}{2}$

per cent. is imposed, and lo! away and upward flies their cost, English and foreign alike. And so another lift is given to the average cost of life, and every one revises his calculations, and with a wry face cuts down his little luxuries. And the rich man finds that £10,000 a year will serve him only where £7,000 served him before, and the poor clerk and the needy governess pinch and starve, and the workman can buy for 20s. what he bought before for 15s., and the man out of work? well, he, poor fellow! has death or the workhouse. And for what? To obey an Imperial Instinct, to fulfil an Imperial Destiny, to yoke ourselves to our brothers beyond the seas, to strike the foreigner at last a blow of vengeance. Oh, God-given Instinct! oh, Glorious Destiny! Oh, Noble Patriotism! Oh, Statesmanship long-sighted and profound!

THE FIFTH LETTER

SIR,—In this letter I shall treat of the special object of your hatred. If there is a thing you distrust and utterly abhor, it is a manufactured import. To raw materials, especially to such articles as cotton, wool, flax, and the other products of hot climates, you extend a chilly condescension ; but you turn your back on finished articles not made by British hands. In your eyes every sheet of glass, every box of tools, every ton of made iron, every machine, every sheet of paper, every door and window frame, every pound of cement, every bottle of chemicals, is a nail in our industrial coffin and a malignant effort to carry our commercial fortress. And yet are not three things perfectly clear to the simple intelligence ? First, that the proportion of the manufactured things we import is as nothing to the volume of the goods which we make at home, and that the number of hands permanently thrown out of employment by such imports is not visible to the naked eye. In 1904 we imported £135,000,000 of manufactured goods, of which a great proportion are materials for more finished articles which we make to sell at home or to export.

Secondly, that small as is this proportion, it is precisely the importation of competitive articles which keeps the prices of English-made things within a moderate limit. Prohibit the import of paper, of window frames, of silk goods, of boiler plates, of wire rods, of steam engines, of what you will, and you will see a remarkable thing—an instant rise in the price of the home-made thing for no apparent reason. You will see, too, a less sudden but a certain rise in all allied trades from sympathy and material necessity. It is our free imports which make monopolies impossible. Reduce imports by taxing them, and each upward movement of their value makes easier the way of the monopolist and the trust-monger. ·

Thirdly, if we can obtain from the foreigner finished materials for our trade at a low price, and can thus find work for our more highly-skilled artisan, would you forbid us to buy abroad that which we can obtain better and less dearly than at home? Will you not rather allow that there is reason in the theory that a wise man confines himself to the work he can do best, and should obtain from every quarter the materials which he can make into a higher and more finished form?

Adam Smith puts the whole matter into a few sentences, pregnant with wisdom and common sense :—

"It is the maxim of every prudent master of a family never to attempt to make at home what it will cost him more to make than to buy. . . . What is prudence in the conduct of every private family can scarce be folly in that of a great kingdom. If a foreign country can supply us with a commodity cheaper than we ourselves can make it, better buy it of them, with some part of the produce of our own industry employed in a way in which we have some advantage."

No one has preached with clearer emphasis than you the doctrine of the open door. For what did we send a " mission " to Tibet if it was not to break down her wall of exclusion, and if she is to be punished for refusing to receive our imports, how will you defend your own hatred of foreign goods? This dread of imports which besieges you, this fallacy of self-containment which fascinates you, this dogma that no one should allow another to contribute to the work he does, is the old superstition which drove the mobs of a century ago to destroy the machinery which in their eyes was taking the bread from their mouths. If you shut out imports, which are the foundation of the more finished things which our workmen turn out, you are not giving more work to those at home. You are reducing the amount of work which can be profitably done, and you are reducing the number of English workmen who can find employment. Did you read a few months ago the pathetic case of the amiable but reactionary clergyman who was haled before a magistrate for an assault in a London market? Asked the reason of his violence, he answered that the assaulted man was using a barrow, and by such use was depriving another man of the work which he might have found if manual labour had not been ousted by the barrow. You smile at the act and the inference. But what of your own theories of employment? *De te fabula narratur.*

This, then, we must endeavour to see clearly. To raise the price of a foreign article is to raise the price of the English article of the same grade. To produce such a rise is to tax the whole of our industrial system. You cannot place a duty on any single thing which enters into an English manufacture of wide use without fining every manufacturer of every possible article, without thereby increasing the cost of living to rich and poor, without lowering the general scale of wealth and comfort, without reducing our export trade, and without impoverishing the state and the nation.

It may be true that a duty on cement alone, or on steel alone, or on paper alone, or on any *one* article would not throw the whole of our trade and commerce into confusion. And so the cutler thinks that he will escape the general increase of expense, and the paper-maker that his trade will not be affected so long as universal import duties are not imposed. He forgets that in the hurly-burly of the tariff each trade will fight for its own protection, and that, as each trade will certainly win its case, the resultant rise will in due course affect the business of the cutler and the paper-maker, and the domestic out-goings of both. There will come the inevitable sequel—lower profits and an urgent and irresistible demand for a higher tariff, bringing with it a further rise and a further impoverishment.

Once admit Protection, and you cannot restrict it to one industry. It will be claimed by every manufacturer. The history of tariffs has been uniform. It begins with a small and plausible tax, then the circle widens until it includes all the trades whose wealth and organization give them the power to enforce their claims. At first, each industry fights for itself, and opposes the grant of Protection to another trade. But the cement-maker quickly finds that the jealousies of other trades are too strong, that its own influence is insufficient to maintain a monopoly of tariff privilege. Then " log-rolling " comes in, and the organization of the individual industry is extended to a wider combination of industries, allied for the purpose of continuing or enlarging the tariff.

This, too, you must not fail to notice. A small duty of 5 per cent. or 10 per cent., is useless as a protection, because it would not make imported articles prohibitively dear, and it would not be effective. It would indeed raise the cost of living, but it must soon give way to a duty of double or three times the amount. How can you, with a 10 per cent. tariff, " retaliate " on a foreign country which puts 25 per cent. to 50 per cent. on your goods ? Is it not a popgun against a man-of-war ?

You will say that the picture is grossly exaggerated, that your design is misinterpreted, and that you would except the more important manufactured imports which are useful or necessary to our own trades. But again I answer : You will find your hands tied and bound. If you put a duty on foreign cement, you will obviously raise the price of home-made cement, and thereby the cost of building. And if you say, "I will stop here," how will you be able to resist the demands of the paint-maker, the screw-maker, the cutler, the chemical manufacturer, the glue-maker, the tool-maker, the frame-maker ? Are they to see the cement-maker protected and themselves open to the attacks of the foreign under-seller ? What appeals of " ruined " trades will assail your ear ; what denunciations, what lobbyings, what pressure on your Parliamentary supporters ? You have set out on the incline, and to the bottom you must go.

Of manufactured imports there remain things domestic and luxurious, and on these I shall ask you to reconsider your views. It may be difficult to distinguish between the two classes, but you will agree that though hats and bonnets and shirts and woollen and linen articles and soaps and matches are not absolutely necessary to the existence of a human being, life would be less genial without them. On the other hand, books, and champagne, and jewels, and fancy articles, and lace and motors, and tobacco, and musical boxes, and silks, and furs, and watches and clocks, are perhaps not necessary for life, and we will look upon them as luxuries. Now, of the former class we import about £27,000,000, and of luxuries, say, £28,000,000.

I would call your attention to two points here. Of the former things, many of which compete with our home-made articles, we only import £27,000,000, and of this we re-export over £2,000,000. Now, will you seriously urge that so small a list, so small an amount, can make any vital difference to the vast total of our home trade? Think for a moment of the gigantic volume of domestic articles turned out by English workmen for English use, and then tell me in what way these imports of things can bring to ruin our manufactures, advancing as they do each year to a higher level of wealth? We are not hurting our own people by our imports, we are adding to our national wealth by moderation in expenditure : we are (surely this will appeal to you) forcing the absurd foreigner to sustain us in cheap comfort, and, what is very much to the purpose, we are keeping the prices of the home-made goods to a moderate and possible level. No! we are not doing this at the cost of our own workmen, and this I shall show you in another letter.

The last class of imported goods we have named luxuries, and on some of those which are not already taxed you may, if you please, place a duty, because, in the first place, it will be paid by those who can afford to pay it ; and, secondly, such a duty will not in most cases be protective. For, as we cannot ourselves produce the most luxurious things, we shall not be raising at the same time the cost of the home-made article. But I would ask you to deal gently with them, and only to tax moderately, because if you place a heavy duty on a luxury, the taxpayer will, consciously or unconsciously, reduce his expenditure in some other direction, and such economy may bear hardly on our home trade. You will not keep out luxuries, and you will merely reduce the spending power of the public.

We have now finished our consideration of imports, and I have laid to rest, I hope, some of the fears which harass your mind. Let us now sum up the case, and see whether the total is more alarming than its component parts. Here, then, is the official table of all our imports and exports from foreign countries and our Colonies during the year 1904 :—

BRITISH IMPORTS AND EXPORTS IN 1904.

	Imports (c.i.f.)*	Exports (f.o.b.)†
	£	£
Food, Drink, and Tobacco ...	231,790,837	16,926,051
Raw and semi-raw materials ...	182,210,518	35,670,495
Manufactures	135,150,692	243,942,434
Miscellaneous	2,210,077	4,278,917
Totals	£551,362,124	£300,817,897

You will hear, I doubt not with astonishment, that of our vast imports no less than about 80 per cent. were foodstuffs and raw or semi-raw materials. If you place a duty on these things, you will, without the shadow of a doubt, place an intolerable burden on a whole people. You will lower its food standard, impair its physique and its morals, and lessen its comforts. Under pretence of helping its workmen you will make a few men wealthier and the masses poorer. You will, if you tax manufactured materials, place a burden not less heavy on its industries. You will increase the cost of every material of trade, you will reduce the consumption of food and manufactures at home and their export abroad, and you will prevent our merchants from competing on favourable terms with their keen and jealous rivals in the markets of the world.

If you place a duty on domestic articles, you will increase their price, whether they be imported from abroad or made at home. You will therefore reduce the amount of purchases and the volume of trade. If you tax luxuries, you will, by reducing the amount imported, reduce the value of your taxes to a sum little more than the expense of collecting it.

See what a load you will place on our shoulders. Your 10 per cent. on our £120,000,000 of manufactured imports will probably raise their price by at least 8 per cent. But this is not all or nearly all. Our annual consumption of goods manufactured in Britain is valued at over £600,000,000. Your import duty will drive the price of these up to the same height, and you

---

* c.i.f. = cost, insurance, and freight.
† f.o.b. = cost of the goods delivered *free on board*.

will add another £48,000,000 to the cost of living. This is the
sum :—

10 per cent. on manufactured imports	£12,000,000
Consumers' loss on £120,000,000 at 8 per cent.	£10,000,000
Consumers' loss on £600,000,000 at 8 per cent.	£48,000,000

or a loss to the public of nearly £60,000,000, against a gain
to the Treasury of £12,000,000. Again I ask, is this business?

THE SIXTH LETTER

OF EXPORTS

SIR,—We have now arrived at that branch of our commerce which alone fascinates you, and whose increase or decrease fills you with wild joy or morbid fear. I have already said that your whole attitude is mistaken, that our exports have not decreased, but have wonderfully increased, that our home trade is far more important than our exports, and that both our home trade and our exports would collapse without the aid of our imports. Again, let me repeat, commerce is exchange. Every import, which seems to you to displace an honest British worker, is in reality finding work for him, because as we must pay for our imports, and as we do not pay in money, it is obvious that we can only pay by an export of some kind.

Now let us see how our export trade stands, its value and its progress. In the last letter you will find a simple table of our exports and imports during the year 1904. Of food, you see, we exported but a paltry fraction of the amount which we bought, and that you will allow is very natural. A rich country, like a rich individual, has no time to grow its own food, and, if it had the time, often it has not the land. You will notice that the exports of jams and confectionery form an important factor, but, alas, they will decrease. Why? Because, in your zeal for the West Indian planters, you have prevented the importation of cheap sugar from Russia and Argentina, have thus raised enormously the price of sugar, and will make it impossible for our manufacturers to export cheaply and to beat the foreigner in his own market.

Raw and semi-raw materials are valued at £35,000,000, and of this coal accounts for £26,000,000. We also re-export foreign and colonial materials, for which we have become a market through our open ports. We import, probably in British ships, such things as copper ore, flax and hemp, furs and wool, and send them forth, again probably in British ships, at an enhanced price. We make both a profit on the goods and a double earning in freight for our ships. You are concerned about our exports of coal. Coal is, you say, an asset, short-lived and destructible, which should be retained in the kingdom and not sent abroad to help the foreigner to work his machinery or his battleships against the foolish Briton. Your alarm seems out of place. Our coal will last us many centuries, and only a dreamer will forbid us to use the main necessity of our industry, because in 500 years our coal may have shrunk to a thousand tons. Much will happen before then, and science may have many surprises for us. Your other fear is vain. As Mr. Thomas has shown, no foreigner will beat us with our own coal, because our formidable rivals possess the coalfields which make them rich and formidable. The manufacture goes to coal, and not the coal to the manufacture. Half our exported coal goes to feed our own ships which plough the seas, carrying backwards and forwards to every nation from every shore goods with great profit to British shipowners. And is not exported coal a manufacture, the product of well-paid industrial labour and rich capital?

Of manufactured things and materials we imported £135,000,000, most of which we applied to the manufacture of more finished goods Of completely finished things for private use and luxury we imported no more than £55,000,000 worth. Our exports of manufactures, on the other hand, for 1904 are valued at £243,000,000. Even you will allow that if the foreigner dumped his goods on us, we paid him back with compound interest. We are the great exporters of the world. But, in reality, as I have shown you before, the figures of these exports are, except in the cotton industry, as nothing to the immense proportions of our home trade. The annual output of finished goods in Great Britain has been increasing each year for half a century, and approaches the gigantic sum of £900,000,000. Against this mighty total we imported

only £115,000,000 in 1904. You will not find here a proof
that our manufactures have been slain by the competition or
the tariffs of the foreigner. Unless, therefore, you insist that
nothing shall enter England which can be made by her sons,
you can find little to fill a reasonable man with uneasy
suspicion. Our manufactures are increasing, our wealth is
increasing, and because our imports are increasing our home
trade and our exports grow.

That our export trade has suffered from Protective tariffs is
an undoubted fact, and that it has suffered more than the
export trades of Germany and the United States is also true.
But in this there is nothing sinister. We are the great
exporters of manufactured articles, and a manufacturing nation
of necessity will feel Protective tariffs more than a food-
exporting nation. As a matter of fact, Germany has suffered
in its exports of manufactured goods almost as severely as
ourselves.

Let us now consider the growth of these exports, and see
whether it is as slow as you fear and as disproportionate to
the growth of the commerce of other nations. I quote your
own words :—

"What is my case ? What are the arguments by which I
support it ? What are the objections of my opponents?
Well, my case is that the trade of this country as measured—
and I think it ought to be mainly measured—by the exports of
this country to foreign countries and to British Possessions,
has, during the last twenty or thirty years, been practically
stationary, that our export trade to all those foreign countries
which have arranged tariffs with us has enormously diminished,
and at the same time the exports to us have enormously
increased."

"What are the facts ? The year 1900 was the record year
of British trade. The exports were the largest we have
ever known. The year 1902—last year—was nearly as
good, and yet if you will compare our trade in 1872, thirty
years ago, with the trade of 1902—the export trade—you
will find that there has been a moderate increase of twenty-two
millions. That, I think, is something like 7¼ per cent."

In answer to this let me advance a few figures. I give you
the annual value of our exports for certain years from the
year 1870.

					£ Million.
1870	...	...	...	...	200
1871	...	...	...	...	223
1872	...	...	...	...	256
1873	...	...	...	...	255
1874	...	...	...	...	239
1884	...	...	...	...	233
1894	...	...	...	...	216
1904	...	...	...	...	301

Increase of 1904 over 1872, £45,000,000.

Now on this I would remark two things: (1) that our exports, even taken at present values, can hardly be said to have remained stationary. You have, allowing for periods of depression, a steady increase from £200,000,000 to £301,000,000; (2) that 1872 was obviously an exceptional year, compared with the years which preceded and followed it; (3) that it is absurd to contrast two periods without taking into account the enormous difference in the purchasing power of money. From 1870, there has been a fall of prices averaging 50 per cent. This you know full well. In 1881, when you were President of the Board of Trade, a similar threnody was sung over the decay of British trade, and you were not slow to pour fine scorn upon it, justly saying that to compare two values and to say nothing about the fall in prices was ridiculous and insincere. If, then, we compare our exports in 1872 and 1904, making allowance for this fall, we arrive at a conclusion totally different from yours, and one vastly encouraging.

			Value given in Trade Returns. £ Million.		Value based on Prices of 1873. £ Million.
1872	...	...	255	...	256
1904	...	...	301	...	453

Real increase of 1904 over 1872, £197,000,000.

Here, then, from 1872 to 1904, you have a real export increase of £197,000,000, or of 78 per cent. compared with a growth of population of only 30 per cent. Does this show stationary trade?

The fact is that by choosing a year here and a year there, by taking a good year as your starting point and a bad one as your closing point, it is possible to prove anything. Now I wish to put a plain question to you. Why did you choose the year 1872 as your year of reference? Did you choose it because it was a year of dear coal, of high prices, of artificial inflation, of abnormal prosperity, a year in which the close of the Franco-German War allowed or forced both combatants to purchase enormously in our markets to repair the waste of war? Why did you not take the year 1875, when prices had fallen again and the value of the export trade had been reduced to a normal level? Did you presume on the short memory and the ignorance of the British public, or did you really forget your own refutation of 1881? Is this worthy of an English statesman?

The exposure of this elementary error will make us receive with caution your lamentation over our decreasing trade with Protected countries. We send, you say, £42,500,000 of manufactures less to them than we did in 1872. The same choice of 1872-3 vitiates your argument, and the same neglect of falling prices turns your position. Take a normal year, and you will find that to these countries with their tariff walls and all their foolish and extravagant apparatus of Protection, we are sending nearly 50 per cent. more than we sent thirty years ago. You will see that the increase in our exports is nearly all manufactured goods, and that the increase in our imports is nearly all food and raw material.

One more statement I will examine. You ask us to give a preference to the Colonies and to shut out the foreigner because, you say, our foreign exports are decreasing and our Colonial exports are growing fast. I have shown you that your first claim is unfounded, and your second has no greater value. The proportion between our foreign and our Colonial exports has been fairly constant for many years, and, taking 100 points as a standard, has averaged 65 to foreign countries and 35 to the Colonies. This proportion was only disturbed by the South African War of 1899-1902. If you will examine the export tables, you will see that the munitions of war and the materials for restocking the devastated republics enormously increased the value of our exports, raising the Colonial proportion to 37 and 38 in 1901 and 1902. But see what follows. The unnatural expansion is over with the war, and in 1903 the foreign exports increase far more rapidly than the Colonial, while in 1904 the movement is still more marked. Here are figures :—

	To Foreign Countries. £	To British Possessions. £
1902	174,300,000	109,100,000
1903	179,600,000	111,100,000
1904	188,800,000	112,000,000

In three years our foreign exports have increased by £14,500,000, while our Colonial exports have only increased by £2,900,000.

A glance at the following table will show you that we are not doing so badly—even if you compare us with your miracles of success :—

TOTAL EXPORTS PER HEAD OF POPULATION.

Average of decade.	United Kingdom. £ s. d.			United States. £ s. d.			Germany. £ s. d.			France. £ s. d.		
1873—1882 ...	11	5	4	2	18	7	3	19	1	4	11	10
1883—1892 ...	10	17	7	2	12	3	3	13	4	4	10	4
1893—1902 ...	11	11	4	3	2	6	4	8	3	4	5	9

TOTAL EXPORTS PER HEAD, AT PRICES OF 1873.

Year.	United Kingdom. £ s. d.			United States. £ s. d.			Germany. £ s. d.			France. £ s. d.		
1873	11	9	8	3	2	4	4	9	1	4	3	2
1883	14	13	6	3	17	1	4	6	8	6	6	5
1893	15	14	11	4	0	8	5	17	3	6	1	4
1902	18	17	8	5	6	1	7	3	10	6	1	7
Increase of 1902 over 1873 ...	7	8	0	2	3	9	2	14	9	1	18	5

The truth is that our exports are far greater in proportion to our population than the exports of any nation in the world. We have a population a little larger than that of France, and we export £120,000,000 worth more. Our population is nearly 20,000,000 less than that of Germany, and we export

£50,000,000 worth more. Our population is half that of the United States, and our export trade is equal to hers.

You cannot prevent these unequal movements of commerce. Go to Bradford, and you will find a weaving industry "crippled" together with comfort and prosperity. Why? Because the workmen, choosing higher forms of industry with the certainty of better wages, have left the lower forms to those who will take less wages. Do you think the aggregate prosperity of Bradford is less than it was? It is not. Foreign demand, like the home demand, is always shifting. Every trader knows the instability of fashion, and if you will examine and tabulate the output of any British firm, you will be astonished at its variable nature. One year our worsted goods may suit the foreigner better than French goods, and Bradford rejoices. Another year the rage or the climate is all for cotton goods, and Manchester triumphs. One year the cost of an article is low, and its export increases ; another year labour or materials are dear, and the export diminishes.

Do not, I beg, identify prosperity with exports. It is activity or slackness in the home trade which brings prosperity or distress. Even while the wealth of a nation grows, and its internal trade rapidly increases, its export trade may slacken. The home consumer, earning more money, can buy more goods, whether made at home or abroad. More attention will be given therefore to the manufacture of goods for home markets. In the natural order of things there will be a diminished export to the countries whose progress in civilization enables them to make what before they had to buy. But there need be no alarm so long as the home trade is prosperous. Let that be your first consideration.

On the other hand, an increase in export trade is sometimes an index of decreased prosperity. When a man cannot sell his goods by the ordinary channels he seeks new ones even if they be more difficult ; and a trader who finds a smaller demand at home, ships his goods at a lower price to be sold abroad. This is the real cause of dumping, and such export is a sign of weakness rather than of strength. If you wish for a proof of this, I ask you to turn to the tables of Trade for 1904, where you will see that in the last months of the year a rapid increase in the exports is accompanied by an increasing dearth of employment.

The history of our trade is one of decennial periods—prosperity and inflation—depression and panic—slow recovery—convalescence and prosperity. You cannot have in this world an even and equable procession of events. Generations come and go, new men and new inventions rise, new fashions conquer. The same thing which delighted our fathers delights us no longer, and our sons will scorn our wares. No good trader is amazed if one section of his business declines through age or competition ; resourceful and alert, he marks out new lands for conquest ; forgetting what lies behind and buried, he presses forward to another mark. It is eager skill and not Protection which brings success.

We are then forced to three conclusions:—(1) that the export trade is useless as an index of prosperity unless the home trade is also prosperous; (2) that an increase of imports is a sign of growing wealth, and conversely that their decrease is a sign of growing poverty; (3) that the rapid increase in the exports of Germany and the United States will gradually slacken as their wealth grows and the demands of their home trade increases.

Where we have been beaten, where foreign imports have ousted our own goods, whether in Britain or in foreign countries, the victory of the foreigner has been won by brains, by skill, by technical training, and excellence. This you will see in the decadence of some sections of our pottery trade, where we hold the worn-out designs and methods of a century ago good enough for the foreign buyer, who has all the charm and skill and novelty of the French and German potters at his beck and call. The lesson which we learn on every side is one and the same. Tariffs cannot kill a healthy trade; it will climb over any wall. Our export trade, our imports, the successes of the foreigner, the rise and fall of industries, the ebb and flow of trade—all teach us that the success of a man, of a firm, of a nation, comes from character, from skill, from energy, from trained intelligence, from efficiency, from method, from organization and adaptability.

The British merchant and manufacturer has become torpid and conservative ; spoiled by wealth, he loves overmuch his ease, affects to sneer at new methods and technical advance. He finds his business harder to win ; rivals creep up ; things passing his comprehension become the established vogue, and he curses the foreigner. Let him rather search the horizon, seek fresh markets, renew his machinery, adapt himself to new conditions, and learn the new knowledge.

In truth, all the devices and tariffs and nostrums in the world will not permanently change the direction of trade. A good business man will send his goods everywhere in spite of vexatious and temporary obstacles. You cannot alter the fact that over 60 per cent. of our export trade, and 80 per cent. of our import trade, is done with foreign nations, and will you be so reckless as to risk, nay, to suffer, the thousand losses which will follow the dislocation of so vast a commerce, in the hope of gaining a few pounds from the Colonies? How much we can lose is a point which shall be discussed in my ninth letter.

Meantime let me end this one by quoting to you one of your own stories, and I hope you will not accuse me of striking a note too personal. You were, we all know, in earlier years a successful maker of screws, and from your experience in this industry you once drew an effective argument against Protection. You told your audience how, in spite of an American tariff of 100 per cent., and of high duties in other countries, in spite of the fact that foreign screws were dumped free into Great Britain, your screws entered the ports of our rivals and ousted the screws protected by high tariffs. Such terror did you inspire in your competitors that the manufacturers of the United States, impotent with all their duties against the Free Trade screw, were forced to pay you an annual subsidy so that you should refrain from importing your screws into the United States, and all the time your workmen were earning higher wages and working less hours than in the factories of France and Germany. The American consumer, you showed, was forced not only to pay a monstrous price for his screws, but it was from his pocket that the American manufacturer drew the subsidy by which to induce you to keep your Free Trade screws out of the American market.

This is an admirable reminiscence, and it seems as apt now as it was in 1885. Do you propose to re-write the story, and point another moral?

THE SEVENTH LETTER

SIR,—What is "to dump"? It is a new word in our dictionary, and yet it is a word in all men's mouths. Sinister it is to you, and maleficent is its motive. Let us see whether the reality is equal to the picture it calls up. To dump, let us say, is to place suddenly and at a low price much stock on a market, and thereby to reduce the current price of the article dumped. In your eyes there is added an odious meaning to this action, for the foreign dumper ever sells below cost price. His design is to wreck the British market, and to take possession of our ruined stalls. It is a lurid imagining, and it might very well give us grave material for thought if it were not overstrained.

To dump is in reality the natural policy which every progressive business at intervals adopts. Manufacturers in their anxiety for a possible demand, or in their desire to take advantage of cheap materials, are often guilty of making more goods than they require. They find they are overstocked; they have locked up too much capital in articles which will not improve by keeping. They sell off their surplus. The draper has his clearance sales or his "bankrupt stocks," the publisher sells his remainders, the ironmaster his surplus iron and steel. There is no reason to doubt that the sudden forcing of such stock on a market, whether it be strong or falling, has a prejudicial effect on its stability, and may jeopardize the safety of weak traders. But this is a drawback of trade, and no one to-day proposes to forbid a clearance sale because the small draper round the corner, or even the big one in the next street, may have to reduce his prices for a few weeks. Nor does any one seriously believe that the draper sells his surplus stock in order to crush his rivals. A similar set of circumstances governs dumping in international affairs. In a Protectionist country, where high tariffs favour the creation of huge trusts and monopolies which can enforce their own price on the consumers of that country, it often happens that a period of inflated prosperity is followed by a period of serious depression and semi-panic. The great trusts suddenly find that the purchasing power of the public has disappeared, and they are left with a heavy surplus of the article which they make. They will not lower the price in their own country lest they break the "ring," but they export it to other countries at a far lower price than they will sell it at home.

Now see the result of this. They find their most ready buyers in the countries which have no tariff, such as England, or a low tariff, such as Belgium. The English and the Belgian engineer buys the iron or steel cheaply, makes machinery at a moderate cost, and sells it in the dumping country at a lower price than that at which an engineer in that country can make it.* Is not this to be hoist with one's own petard?

In your dread of this policy of foreign manufacturers you make one considerable mistake. You say that every other country but England has imposed a special tariff to meet dumped goods. This is not correct. No country has imposed such a tariff. If you will make inquiries, you will find that cheap German steel has been dumped not only into Free Trade England, but has passed through the Protectionist tariffs of Austria, Switzerland, and the United States. Nor can you point out a single industry which has been ruined by dumping. You generalize with safety, but when you proceed to seek for an example, you beat the air. I shall at the end of this letter examine the patients whom you have

---

* "German papers report that an English firm has been awarded the contract for a large gasometer, by the city of Copenhagen, being the lowest bidder—53,185 dollars ; the lowest German bid was 54,742 dollars. The curious part is that the English firm intends to use German material, finishing it in England. It will be bought in Germany at export prices, which are about cost or even less. The German manufacturers of gas reservoirs cannot purchase their raw material in Germany as cheaply as foreign firms can, and therefore cannot compete with English manufacturers."—*U.S. Consul*, 1903.

condemned to premature death, and I believe we shall be able
to pronounce them robust and prosperous.

Mr. Law expresses hot indignation that a German steel
maker should sell his dumped goods in the English market at
£4 10s. per ton while he charges his own consumer £6 10s.
a ton. Mr. Law fails to see two things :—(1) That the Free
Trade Englishman, taking advantage of the folly of the Protectionist foreigner, buys at a low price the material which
he can send back into the country of its origin at a profit.
(2) The unhappy German public is obliged under a Protectionist
régime to pay nearly 50 per cent. more for its goods than the
Englishman. In other words, the German buys dear and sells
cheap, while the Englishman buys cheap and sells dear. Can
you ask for a more cogent or a more pithy condemnation of
Protection ?

Your assumption that the foreigner is actuated by a malevo-
lent desire and design to ruin our industry by his dumped
goods is unfounded. Men cannot continue to sell goods,
especially manufactured goods, below their cost : only one end
awaits such action. They may in untoward circumstances be
compelled so to sell, but it is a forced sale, a result of depression and crisis, of a financial and commercial disaster of
which a Free Trade country, with no unhealthy and artificial
inflation, has little experience.

Let me make this concession. If it could be proved that
another nation or a foreign trust with illimitable resources
had set its mind on the ruin of a British trade by dumping at
half the cost price, I would allow that a serious situation had
arisen. But in the first place a stringent proof would be
necessary that an evil motive was there ; and, secondly, we
should have to assure ourselves that an act of retaliation
would cure and not inflame the wound. Every other industry would call for a like favour, and you could not resist
the pressure. Again, a moderate tariff would not exclude
goods dumped with such a motive, and if you place a high
tariff on such goods, you double the cost of the home-made
article or material, and your original suffering is but a pale
shadow of your second state.

The fact is that in proportion to the output of a country, the
amount of goods which it dumps (i.e. sells below or almost
below cost) is minute. To the morbid imagination of a timid

manufacturer such an importation assumes a portentous guise, but let him take; heart of grace. No British industry has closed its doors through foreign dumping. Rather does it flourish on the dump.

Let us now await with sad eyes the long and melancholy procession of industries and trades—once the glory of our race, now, alas! shattered and slain by the impious hand of the importer. The catalogue is long, indeed, and terror-inspiring. At the head comes Iron, then Cotton passes, then Shipping, then Agriculture, then Tin-plates; then file by in pathetic array Silk and Glass and Alkali and Wire and Cycles and Watches and Straw Hats and Jewellery; and then, most piteous of all, Pearl Buttons. Sugar shall end the line.

Iron, the greatest of our industries, is, if the figures of the trade and our own export figures are to be trusted, in the most robust health and in no need of any patent medicine. Its figures are prodigious. It is calculated that the value of iron and steel products of the United Kingdom is £160,000,000. Against this we imported in 1904 in a rough or half-finished state £8,000,000 worth of iron and steel, and £8,000,000 of machinery, tools, and hardware—in both cases an amount incapable of causing more than a small and temporary depression in the trade. And place against such a depression the enormous advantages of a supply for our manufacturers of cheap raw material. By its aid we can make machinery at such a price that we supply the home market with cheap iron and steel goods and beat the foreigner with manufactures forged out of his own materials. In truth, the industry advances in wealth, and if 1904 does not overtop 1903 you must remember that its prosperity is won in the most adverse circumstances, amid the poverty and depression which came from your war in South Africa. What figures shall we show when a prudent Government shall at length check the ruin of our finances?

Of Cotton I need say little. The looms are all roaring full time, and the men of Lancashire are as disinclined for your schemes as the forgers of iron and the makers of steel. In 1904 we exported a record quantity of cotton piece-goods. If you wish to know how Protection chains and makes impotent a strong nation, you have no clearer evidence than the cotton manufacture of the United States. How comes it that British spinners, forced to rely on foreign cotton, transported at great cost over 3,000 miles of sea, make cotton goods so cheaply that they almost monopolize the markets of the world ?   How comes it that the nation which grows the cotton, which can make it into goods with every advantage of nature, is unable to compete with us in the industry which should be hers by right ?   It is, you know, because she permits the infamous coils of Protection to strangle her.

Of shipping I shall in another letter write at length, and though the splendid story would bear repetition, I will not ask you to listen twice to the refutation of your fallacies. When I say that we own about one-half of the world's shipping and are increasing the disproportion, I think I may assert, without fear of retort, that the only danger which shipping dreads is the return of the Protection which has ruined the American merchant fleet, and which, by reducing the imports and the exports, would quickly ruin ours.

In direct contradiction of your gloomy pessimism we shall find that the growth of our merchantmen is as steady as the keenest patriot might desire.   Here is a comparative statement of British and American ships employed in the direct trade between the United Kingdom and the United States :—

	1860	1880	1900
Great Britain	3,940,000 tons	6,939,000 tons	10,162,000 tons
United States	2,245,000 „	1,442,000 „	1,035,000 „

Do these figures confirm your misery ?   And even if foreign fleets did increase a little more quickly than British building, can you wonder at a natural event, and how will Protection help you ?   How rather will it not intensify the malady ?

In Agriculture we have at last found an industry which Free Trade has not made prosperous.   But to the reproaches of the landlord we return a quick answer : Cheap bread is a greater good than high rents.

The history of agriculture after the abolition of the Corn Laws—a measure assumed to be fatal to that industry—was for thirty years one of increasing prosperity. The enormous growth of our manufactures and commerce, due to free imports, and the growth of the national wealth brought a corresponding increase in the value of land. The landlord raised his rents and the labourer his wages. Then came a change. The vast new area of wheat land in America—producing the finest corn with small need of capital and unburdened by heavy rents—brought about the inevitable result. Foreign wheat was imported in enormous volume, and, aided by rapid and cheapened transport, entered into serious and fatal rivalry with the produce of land exhausted by centuries of harvests. The farmer, confronted by this overwhelming competition, had to face another trouble. The labourers, attracted by the pleasures and the higher wages of the town, began to desert the countryside, or could only be prevailed to remain by the promise of increased earnings. Changing conditions had to be met by new methods. The dearth of men was to some extent balanced by the use of modern machinery, and the decreasing profits of wheat-growing were redressed by the increasing profits of stock-rearing and dairy-farming. Three million acres were withdrawn from the area of arable land and added to the area of grass land, but the aggregate area of cultivated land has not diminished ; nay, it has increased. The farmer has taken to the rearing of horses, the breeding of stock, and the marketing of dairy produce.

Nor is it so certain that the position of agriculture is as disastrous as you imagine. The decrease in the acreage of arable land, though large, is not enormous, and is met by the increase of pasture. The reduction of rents to a moderate figure has assisted the farmer, and the removal of the rigorous and vexatious conditions of hire which embarrass him will assist him still more.

The agricultural interest was grievously wounded by the great fall in values which set in about 1877, but it was the slave of an antiquated system, sinking under semi-feudal conditions, and served by men lacking the energy, the ability and the capital which made the fortunes of the manufacturer. The depression which has ensued is not peculiar to Great Britain ; it has been shared by all the great European nations, and the imposition of duties on wheat has not prevented and cannot cure it. The opening of vast arable areas of virgin soil in the New World is a new factor of invincible force, and we can no more obviate this factor than we can stem the waters of the Atlantic. Nor, it may be added, can we live without imported wheat. There is, however, another side to the medal. We cannot place the interests of any class, important though it may be, against the welfare of a whole nation; and the wealth of landlords and farmers would be dearly bought by the impoverishment and physical deterioration of 40,000,000 of people.

Under Protection the farmer will soon discover that the general rise in the cost of living will more than cover the rise in the price of wheat. Machinery, implements, fodder, feeding-stuffs, will be more costly, his own private expenses will be higher, and when he has paid the higher rent which the landlord will exact there will be little profit left for him. The experience of the German farmer, who, with high Protection, is as poor as he was with low duties, holds little to comfort the British agriculturist.

For the labourer the change has been all for good. Where he was an ill-paid and half-starved serf, he is now well fed and moderately well paid. His wages have risen by 50 per cent., his bread is one-third of the price under Protection, and all the necessaries and many of the small comforts of life are now possible for him.

What shall we say of tin-plates but that they indeed have tested and proved the dogged energy of our race? You would have given up the battle and granted them Protection, but the makers of plates were braver Englishmen. Assailed by foreign duties, they found new markets and in 1904 the industry had the greatest output in its history.

Silk walks next; and even of silk we can speak with hope. It is a trade which has never flourished with a healthy vigour and independence, and even under Protection it took on a sickly air. And yet, even for silk there is a future, for the figures of spun silk show an encouraging upward movement, and join in the conspiracy to prove your figures incorrect.

Of your unhappy reference to Alkali I can only say that it is wrong at all points. This is what you say :—

" In one process for making alkali there are two products—

c

caustic alkali and bleaching powder. People who want to export alkali must make the bleaching powder and get rid of it in order to make it pay. The Germans make as much alkali as they want, and all the bleach that comes in the process they dump here in England. We can only make a limited amount of alkali because we cannot sell our bleach, and if this goes on, we shall sell no alkali at all in that process which requires that both alkali and bleaching should be produced."

We do sell our own bleach, our exports are not on the whole decreasing, and the imports from Germany are minute and not increasing.

Your lamentations over glass are equally wide of the mark. To say that plate-glass once gave employment to 20,000 men when 3000 could easily make all the plate-glass we now import, is really to strain the loyalty of your admirers to breaking pitch. I will not say that glass exports advance by leaps and bounds, but they do advance, and they do not decline. If Germany possesses the sand which glass requires, and can work it at the very doors of her factories, must she not by that very gift of nature have us at a disadvantage? Do you propose to raise the price of every tumbler, and bottle, and wine-glass we use, so that Germany may be made to see that glass sand is not an unmixed good?

But I must pass through your tedious catalogue, and test your figures, always precise and always inaccurate. Cycles dumped down with ruin to our trade? Look at this table, and tell me who is the dumper—England or the foreigner?

Year.			Exports of Cycles.	Imports of Cycles.
1900	...	...	£530,950	£194,848
1901	...	...	577,412	176,355
1902	...	...	718,037	144,535
1903	...	...	849,281	99,027
1904	...	...	740,440	82,784

Let wire, another industry which accepts and thrives on imported iron, tell its own tale in its export figures.

1901	...	...	...	...	...	967,000
1902	...	...	...	...	...	1,043,000
1903	...	...	...	...	...	1,171,000
1904	...	...	...	...	...	1,195,000

Do the symptoms presage an early death ?

A terrible picture you drew in October, 1904, before your Liverpool audience, of American watches dumped in overwhelming and increasing numbers, of an actual living American salesman with 20,000 watches in his boxes to sell at any price. Here are the total figures of our imported watches : you will see that they do not support your gloom.

1901	1902	1903	1904
2,481,329	2,103,115	1,620,619	1,522,126

Straw Hats with pleasant obstinacy belie the figures you quoted at Luton. Foreign hats come in less and the British hat, wanting in charm but alive with energy, advances in vogue.

Of Jewellery your treatment is really delightful. So monstrous is the insolence of the foreigner that in 1902 he sent in to this long-suffering kingdom £170,000 more of jewellery than he received from us. No wonder there arose a cry of *Shame* at such a breach of international and commercial comity. But did you not know that there had been a revolution in Morocco, and that the Sultan, following the example of more humble folk, had pawned his jewels to an English banker for a vulgar advance, which jewels coming as security to England, were duly entered as imports in the trade returns. This you might not have known, but surely you did know that, setting aside the abnormal and needy Sultan, our imports of such wares have been decreasing and our exports growing for three years. So much for jewellery.

And now only Pearl Buttons remain your last hope and support. What a depth of pathos and tragedy is here ! Of the mysteries of pearl buttons I am not competent to speak. But I have no doubt that fashion and the laundress have as much to do with their decline as the malignity of the American. I find little proof in the import returns of a vast dumping of pearl buttons, and are we to slay ourselves for their fine eyes ?

And what of Sugar? Do you wish to find industries which are being ruined, crushed, overwhelmed? Then look to confectionery and mineral waters. Here is distress and ruin, rampant and visible to all. And who has brought it on them? You, Sir, can tell us.

THE EIGHTH LETTER

SIR,—I have shown you how marvellously our export trade has kept its upward movement, and how unfounded are your fears for our industries. Now I must attack another giant fallacy which looms large to all uninstructed minds. You tell us that as our imports vastly exceed our exports, the balance of trade is against us, that we are buying more than we sell, that we are living on our capital. It is a shocking thought, and I do not wonder that you and Mr. Bonar Law, and Mr. Seddon and Mr. Chaplin, and the rest of your distinguished cohort, stand motionless and with blanched cheeks as our unhappy country swiftly nears the rapids. But your fears are superfluous; the adverse balance does not exist. Is it, Sir, really necessary to explain to you the elementary principles of trade? Can it be true that in all your years of public service, with all your experience at the Board of Trade, you still believe that we pay for our imports with gold, just simply as I pay 6s. across the counter for a box of cigarettes? Do you sincerely believe that our exports, as the returns give them, constitute the whole of our earnings, and that our shipowners and our bankers and our private investors are paid nothing for their services? It must be so, I fear, for are you not ever talking of "adverse" balances? and did not Mr. Seddon once chill England to the marrow when he said that we sent every year out of the country "160 million golden sovereigns" to pay for the "adverse" balance? You would not play upon a note which you know to be false, and I shall, then, with some surprise, assume that you and your followers are sincere in your error.

First let us face the "adverse" balance of 1904 and see how we fare.

Imports, c.i.f.	£551,000,000
Exports of British goods, f.o.b. ... ...⎰	£301,000,000
Exports of previously imported goods ... ⎱	£70,000,000
Excess of Imports	£180,000,000

Here we have a balance apparently against us of £180,000,000 and if the balance were anything but a sham one, the prospect of a prolongation of such balances would be heart-breaking. But, happily, I can show you that there is no adverse balance at all, but rather a balance on the right side. The two most delightful instances of unconscious humour in the whole of your campaign have been Mr. Seddon's golden sovereigns and the panic fear which you experienced at Newcastle. You painted in your most melancholy mood a cruel picture of England exhausted by long years of adverse balances, while the imports gradually grew and the exports as gradually decreased until at last everything was imported and the exports were nil. But I must quote you in full. The passage is the most brilliant in the recent annals of political oratory :—

"Let me suppose that by a great and terrible catastrophe every mill in this country was stopped, every furnace blown out, even the blacksmith's shop silenced, that no atom of manufacture was any longer made in Great Britain, that we depended on everything from the foreigner, what would be the result of this calculation? We should have an import as now of £528,000,000, and we should export nothing. We should import £528,000,000, but we should also import for our own home use that which is at present supplied by our home production. . . . Our total import trade would be £1,918,000,000. There would be no export trade, and under the circumstances this calculation (i.e. the Free Trade calculation) would show that we were two and a half times better than we were before."

Now do you really believe that this picture is a possible one? Do you believe that the affection of foreign countries is so great that they would import £1,918,000,000, and receive nothing in return? To be quite frank, does not this picture prove your invincible ignorance of the laws which govern business and the exchange of commodities?

But was it necessary to look to the future when the past would have served your purpose equally well and better? Why speak of ruin to come when we have long been bankrupt debtors? Look at our tables of exports and imports from 1860, and you will see that year by year the "adverse" balance has rapidly grown, that whereas before 1860 it was under £100,000,000, after 1860 it has each year exceeded that amount. And so, horror of horrors, we who fondly believed that we had been growing rich for these fifty years, now find that we have been heaping upon our heads a yearly burden, until we now owe to the foreigner the gigantic sum of over Seven Thousand Five Hundred Millions of pounds. How the illusions fall away as the cold, clear truth comes into sight! Have even you in your deepest gulf of despair, ever imagined such a collapse of British credit? How shall we escape this ruin?

But no sooner has the first shock of panic passed away than prudence whispers, "Can it be true? Can it be that we, held to be so wealthy, are so poor? Can it be that the foreigner, so zealous for our ruin, has suffered us so long to remain his debtor?" Reason says "No." In all transactions the man who sells takes care that the man who buys is able to pay. Otherwise he does not send the goods. If, then, we have imported goods, it is certain we have paid for them. We can only pay in one way—by exports. Let us, then, see if the real confirms the probable.

First let us consider what the terms *exports* and *imports* mean in the case of an individual. An export is clearly that which he gives out in order to gain an import. It may be goods or it may be brains—sometimes it is a mixture of both. Let me take an example which you will understand. A Minister of State exports his services (sometimes invisible) to the State, and is paid £5,000 a year. His imports exceed his visible exports by that sum. Do you assert that there is a balance against that Minister of £5,000 a year? Do you really believe that because we receive more than we give we are being ruined? Put it in another way. A man sends goods worth £2 10s. to London, and he receives goods which he sells for £3 10s. Do you hold that he is the loser? This rough-and-ready parable will give you a glimmer of the truth.

Let me now adapt it to trade and commerce. You will notice that our imports are marked *c.i.f.*, which means *cost* plus *insurance* plus *freight*. From this it is seen that every article imported into this country is valued not only at its actual cost, but that to it is added the charge of the shipper and the premium of the insurance broker. If £10 of iron is sent to us, you may assume that the iron only costs £8, and that the rest is probably earned by British ships and British insurance companies. On the other hand, exports are marked *f.o.b., free on board*. Here you will understand that you must *add* the shipping dues and the insurance fees—chiefly earned by British firms. Thus, to get the simple cost of an article, i.e. the sum paid to the seller, you must in the case of imports deduct a large sum. Do not, also, as a rule, forget to allot the difference as an earning for one of your own countrymen.

I understand that you despise " invisible " exports, and my exposition may seem to you fantastic, but your common sense will force you to allow that it is the simple truth. If, as you say, we are living on our capital, we should be selling our foreign as well as our home securities, and yet you know that our investments in both are increasing. You say that these invisible exports, even if they exist, produce no employment for the workman. Frankly, do you believe that nearly £200,000,000 a year produce nothing for the nation of those who earn this sum? Tell me: should we be as well off if the whole amount were thrown annually into the sea? More than half the world's commerce is carried in British ships, and the same ship takes out our exports and brings back our imports—earning a double fee. It is calculated by the Board of Trade that our ships earn, for their services in freight alone, and omitting the profits of our insurance companies, £90,000,000 a year. Here, then, you have a noble profit, and for this the only way in which we can receive payment is by imports.

I have yet another set of earnings to place against the adverse balance of our imports. We receive every year, from foreign investments, interest and profits which amount to not less than £100,000,000, and these earnings grow each year. There are too the profits made in foreign business by our bankers and merchants, say £20,000,000. Thus, then, from the earnings of our ships, our insurances, our investments, our services as world-bankers, &c., we receive annually not less than £210,000,000, and if you will add this to the visible exports of goods during 1904, the total will stand as follows :—

	£
Exports of goods £371,000,000	} 581,000,000
Exports of services ... 210,000,000	
Imports 551,000,000	

Estimated Excess of Exports £30,000,000

Here is balm for you—a favourable balance, and the chief part of this balance is retained abroad to our credit, increasing annually the debt which the foreigner owes to us. Thus the wealthier we grow the greater value of imports shall we require to pay us for our services.

You will allow that there is some force in these contentions. You cannot dispute my figures, but you shake your head and are still unconverted. You insist that an article imported into England must imply a displacement of British labour, and the loss to the British mechanic of the work and wages which the manufacture of that article at home would have involved. I admit that your theory has a specious attraction, but it is a plausibility and nothing more. It is the old fallacy that imports are hurtful to the home trade, and that in proportion as the imports increase, the workmen must suffer and the number of the unemployed increase. But for every import we must export in payment, and the more we import the more must we export. Foreign customers will not trust us. Now here is an interesting little table which I beg you to study. It shows you the annual value of our imports and the annual percentage of the unemployed for six years :—

			Percentage of Unemployed Members of Trades Unions making Returns.			Imports of Manufactured and Semi-manufactured Goods. Mill. £
1894	...	...	6·9	...	...	101·7
1895	...	...	5·8	...	...	107·7
1896	...	...	3·4	...	...	117·6
1897	...	...	3·5	...	...	123·8
1898	...	...	3·0	...	...	125·1
1899	...	...	2·4	...	...	135·9

This will stagger you, for it shows that as the imports rise so do the unemployed decrease in number. Unhappily, in 1899, a war came upon us, and with it debt and heavy taxation. What happened? Our spending power decreased, we were able to buy less from abroad, the imports rose slowly, and not by leaps and bounds, and the number of the un-employed has increased distressingly.

			Percentage of Trades Unionists Unemployed.			Imports of Manufactured and Semi-manufactured Goods. Mill. £
1900	...	...	2·9	...	...	110·5
1901	...	...	3·8	...	...	109·1
1902	...	...	4·4	...	..	115·1
1903	...	...	5·1	...	...	115·7

Let me confirm this by another piece of arithmetic. In 1904 our increase in manufactured exports is £9,000,000, and our increase in manufactured imports is under £1,000,000. We have "gained," then, as you say, £8,000,000. According to your theory, half this gain has been spent in wages—i.e. £4,000,000. The annual employment of a man at 30s. per week means £78. If, then, you divide the £4,000,000 by £78, you have an increase in the number of employed amounting to more than 50,000. Unfortunately for your theory, the number of unemployed has been increasing weekly. How will you explain it?

Two more points and I have done with this phantom. Firstly, you need not fear the excess of imports over *visible* exports. Every nation, as it prospers, increases its imports, until in time they exceed the exports. You will find that each year the imports of the whole world exceed the whole world's visible exports by over £200,000,000. If you want an example of a nation in which the exports exceed the imports, go to South America; and in the weak states of that continent you will light upon some countries worthy to receive benediction at your hands in that they export more than they import. But will you invest your capital in their securities?

Secondly (and this must surely lull to peace your fears for our vanishing stock of "golden sovereigns"), if the difference between our exports and imports is paid for in money, you will trace the payment in the export of gold and silver for the year. Now look at the figures. In nearly every year we import more gold than we export. In 1904 the "adverse" balance of trade was £180,000,000. We must, therefore, by your theory, have paid for that balance by sending out of the country 180,000,000 "golden sovereigns." Pray look at the imports and exports of bullion for 1904 :—

Imports ...	...	...	...	£45,563,927
Exports ...	...	...	...	£46,302,832

Shall not this be the quietus ?

THE NINTH LETTER

OF PROTECTION AT WORK

SIR,—In this letter I propose to estimate the tax which you desire to place upon our trades and our community. One thing is clear: a rise in the price of food and a rise in the cost of materials means an increase in the cost of every manufacture. None can gainsay this: the two questions we have to answer are: How many of our industries can bear such an increase in the working of their business? and, How will the consequent increase of price affect the demand for our goods? To the individual trader Protection has charms. The rose-grower, angered by the importation of cheap roses from France, may claim a Tariff, and think himself rich if he gets it. He forgets that a thousand other trades will clamour for like privileges, that when everything is protected everything will be dear, and that when everything is dear, roses will be a poor market.

To pass in review all our great industries would be fatiguing, and would perhaps be unnecessary. For of most of them the same thing may be said. If you will compare, for example, our exports in 1904 of wool and worsted yarns to Germany and to our Colonies, you will see that we sent about £4,000,000 to the former, and but a few thousands pounds' worth to the latter. How will Protection benefit the spinners? It will raise the cost, and therefore the price of the yarns. The home demand will be less, and the German demand for dearer goods will be enormously less; and do you suppose that the Colonial demand will increase to compensate for one-twentieth of our loss? You will, too, retaliate on Germany for her duties on our exports by shutting out her " dumped " woollens, and she will answer by shutting out our yarns from which these very "woollens" are made. You will see the admirable regularity with which your scheme works. The effect of a decreased output and turnover conjoined with an increased cost will be quickly seen in the profit and loss accounts of this industry.

On the iron and steel trades your policy will be nothing less than disastrous. I have shown you in another letter the vast proportions of this industry, and how it thrives on the cheap food which our rivals send us to their own damage. Shut out the iron ore of Spain, and the production of our pig-iron will be lamentably reduced. Why should we forbid low-priced materials to enter, when by a turn of the wrist we can make them into something which sells at three times the price? We grow rich because we buy cheap and sell dear.

Here is an industry whose annual value is not less than £160,000,000, and which supports nearly 1,500,000 people. It exports £65,000,000: it imports £16,000,000. Remember that the greater part of these imports consists of materials for the use of our industry, from which it makes a profit. Do you assert that what remains—the purely manufactured imports— can make an appreciable impression on an output so enormous ; and will you, for the sake of a mere suspicion, maim the export trade of one of the chief pillars of our commerce? How will you aid such an industry as this with your tinkerings and your tamperings, your 5 per cent. on pig iron, and your 7½ per cent. on wire rods? Leave it free to follow its own way, and to work out its own salvation, and it will flourish long years after your Tariff Commission shall have melted into the infinite azure of the past.

The same tale is told of Machinery and of all that the engineer makes. Increase his wages bill and the cost of every part and material, and you make it impossible for him to compete abroad with the success which he can now achieve against the tariffs which exist. The margin is small, and if he has to charge £55 for what he sold before at £50, do you not suppose that a shrewd American or German will step in before him with a machine at £53 15s.? If he loses his export trade (which you assert is his chief prop) how is he to live? Is he to recoup himself by charging the home buyer £60? In that case, what will be the effect on our industries of an all-round rise of 20 per cent. in the cost of machinery? Do not you see

that you are, by this one step, increasing the cost of everything — the smallest as well as the greatest — on which
machinery can work? Into what unseen quagmires does your
ignis fatuus lead you? But you will help the engineer by
excluding or fining foreign machinery. What will be the
result? Our manufacturers will be deprived of the foreign
machinery which is essential for their industries—machinery
which we cannot make, and without which they cannot
compete with foreign manufacturers.

What will be another result? The foreigner will retaliate and
lay a higher duty on the £20,000,000 of machinery which we
send him every year. Less chance than ever for the British
engineer to sell his machine even at £55. Then you will out
with your pistol and lay a higher duty on the foreigner's
machines, and he will answer back, and so the merry game
goes on, and all the while every British manufacturer is forced
to pay 40 per cent. more for his machines, and his trade
dwindles and his workmen are discharged ; until the miserable
war ends, as such wars always end, in exhaustion and poverty.

To Cotton your policy will spell increased expenses, a smaller
output, lower profits and lower wages. You say that you will
not tax raw cotton, but when our Colonies can grow cotton
how will you restrain your preferential hand? And even if
you do not place a direct tax on cotton you will burden it in
fifty ways. The increased cost of shipbuilding will make
freights dearer, the rise in the general cost of living, the taxes
on all the materials of building, will raise the cost of factories.
The enhanced prices of machinery, tallow, chemicals, dyes,
leather, flour, and the other components of finished cotton,
will raise the cost of manufacture by 20 per cent. We can
only maintain the greatness of our cotton trade by our ability
to sell lower than our rivals ; what will become of it when we
have to raise our prices by one-fifth?

If you ask for an example of a trade which will suffer a
ruinous loss, with no chance of enjoying a share of protective privileges, the Coal industry will supply you with
one. Here is a trade which needs no protection against
imports, which depends absolutely upon the prosperity of
every industry and the spending powers of the population.
Reduce the output of industries and you reduce their
demand for coal ; reduce exports and imports and you reduce

the demand of the shipper for coal. Raise the cost of living and you raise the price of coal and the cost of everything made and consumed. Raise the cost and you make it impossible for the British trader to sell his goods abroad and the British citizen to live on a small income at home. So things move in their vicious circle, acting and re-acting and inter-acting; the delicate play of balanced forces disturbed by an awkward and reckless hand.

Of Shipping I must write at length. Though you are bold enough to place our shipping in your schedule of decaying commerce, I notice that you handle the greatest of all British industries with uncertain fingers. And this not without reason. For if one thing is certain without the shadow of a doubt it is that Free Trade has made us the greatest maritime nation of the world. We not only rule the seas with our navy, but we dominate the whole world with our merchant ships. North and south, east and west, under tropical sun and icy blizzard, British ships are sweeping every sea, carrying forth our goods, and bringing back from every shore food and treasures for our own islands and for every nation. Compared with the British marine, the other nations sink into poor proportions. Every year our ships grow with an irresistible growth. In 1880 we owned half as many tons again as we owned in 1860, and in 1900 we had increased our tonnage by another 50 per cent. And the ships still come, until in 1904 we owned 10,000,000 tons, while Germany has only 2,200,000 tons, France 1,200,000 tons, and the United States 900,000 tons. There were in December, 1904, under construction in British yards, merchant ships of the tonnage of 1,049,860. In German ports a tonnage of 177,844 is being built ; in American, a tonnage of 48,892. And this is the industry in which you say our rivals are "galloping" after us. My dear Sir ! Add the whole tonnage of the world together, include old sailing hulks and every form of antiquated steamship you can find, and it will not equal in effective tonnage the whole of the British merchant shipping fleet. The foreigner gives a bounty to his shipbuilders to induce them to build vessels, and yet we, with no help but from Free Trade, in ten years have added to our tonnage more than the whole German merchant fleet, and every year we add to our steamships more than the United States possess. Unhappy and decaying race !

Go to any foreign port you will—France, Germany, America, Belgium—you will find that of all the ships that enter that port in any year the majority are owed by an alien nation, and that of those foreign ships the greater number fly the British flag. We carry 60 per cent. of the trade of America and 45 per cent. of the trade of France, and for our services they pay us nobly. We hold the foreigner in fee. But go to British ports, and you will find the very converse. Of every four tons which enter British ports three are carried by British ships.

How are you going to compensate the shipbuilder for a rise of 30 per cent. in the cost of the materials of his industry? And if you do not, how will he build at his old price the busy little tramps which scurry backwards and forwards across the seas, bringing food and wealth to millions? 15,000 of these fly the British flag, but there will not be 10,000 of them when you have killed our shipping, as Protection has killed the shipping of America. There will not be 5,000 of them when you have reduced our foreign trade and we are " self-contained."

Why do we cover every sea with our shipping? Why cannot American shipowners buy and build their ships in America? Why has the German Emperor to bribe his builders with bounties? Because we alone are free. Because our free ships, unburdened by the accursed weight of Protection and corrupt politics, find their way to any harbour, through any obstacles which the folly of man may set against us. Because we alone are wise enough to welcome all the materials which the foreigner can send us—steel and brass, zinc and iron, timber and rope. The foreigners join together to build our ships cheaply for us, and we are not so foolish as to say them nay, or place a duty on their contributions. And thus it comes to pass that we can build for £20,000 a ship which the American would refuse to build for £30,000.* And thus it happens, too, that the ruined

* Read the evidence of these witnesses (two among many) before the U.S. Commission on Mercantile Marine.

Mr. Joseph D. Lee, Assistant-Secretary to the Board of Trade, Portland, Oregon, says :—" Now comes the question of getting it [an efficient merchant marine] under a tariff system. Other things being equal, it is not possible to compete with Free Trade in building and operating ships. I think that has been shown."

Mr. Orcutt, President of the Newport News Shipbuilding and Dry Dock

British shipbuilder can build a battleship in nine months and 20 per cent. more cheaply than those wise men who hold the beneficent creed of the Protectionist. Is it strange that we control the seas? And are you bent on forcing from our hands the very means by which we have achieved our greatness, on ruining the millions of human beings, the seamen, the engineers, the dockers, the stevedores, the clerks, the carriers, the builders and the colliers who depend on this industry for their daily bread?

Your policy will impoverish our railways as it will our shipping. How will they find the old dividends for their shareholders when trade and transport are reduced? How will they find dividends at all when the cost of every item of their industry is increased by 25 per cent.?

Now let me speak of finance and banking. You have not forgotten your chilly reception when, before a picked assembly of the great bankers and merchants of the City of London, you expounded your gospel and bade your hearers to "think imperially." They were indeed thinking; but their thought was of the shattered fabric of British finance, of trade shrinking and banks breaking. They knew, as all but your "reformers" know, that our greatness as a financial nation depends simply and solely on the greatness of our trade, that it is the multiplication of commercial transactions which ensures the corresponding variety of credit dealings and the prosperity of our bankers. Reduce the number of these transactions by reducing the volume of our trade, or by restricting the number of nations with whom we deal, and you thereby reduce the profits of the banker. Choose an average commercial transaction with a foreign customer, and you will see how the tendrils multiply.

London is banker for the whole world, because a bill on London is the most negotiable of all commercial papers, and a foreign merchant will always, *ceteris paribus*, prefer to deal with

Company, says:—"If I were called on to build a tramp, corresponding to a British tramp of 3,000 tons, the material alone going into the tramp would cost 40 per cent. more here than if the vessel were built in Great Britain. Because everything in the way of material entering into the construction of a ship is highly protected here. It is not only the steel that forms the bulk of the vessel that is affected in price. It is every conceivable item that goes into a ship."

a British merchant to whom he can remit in payment with
the least trouble and cost. London is the one free market for
gold ; it is the centre of the world's commerce, the clearing-
house of all nations, and we have come to finance the whole
world. Free Trade enables us to lend cheaply and quickly.
How will our foreign debtors pay their interest to us and
their debts if foreign produce and goods are cut down as you
desire ? They do not, and they cannot, pay us in gold : they
pay us in cargoes. Shut out their imports, and you rob our
investors of their dividends.

There has been no great panic or crisis in our land for near
a score of years. Our finance is stable because Free Trade not
only makes us the bankers of the world, but forbids the false
glory which is shed around the " propositions " of the monopolist syndicates and the inflation of the tariff gambler. See
how strong and steady has been our foothold throughout your
war, and the depression which has followed it. Panic has
reigned in the countries which worship your new god ; but
we, the ruined, pass unscathed through the fire.

On the Home trade your policy will bring ruin. We
have seen how fatal will be your gift to the greater industries. Fatal will it be, too, to the smaller trades and to
the shopman. Increase the cost of food, and what will the
public do ? Food they must have, much or little ; coal they
must have, good or bad ; clothes they must have, fair or
shoddy ; but what of the thousand things which they need
not buy, or can buy at longer intervals ? What of knives and
forks, of scissors and books, of pots and pans, of plates and
glasses, of tea and rice, of calico and needles and cotton, of ink
and paper, of pens and pencils? Here are a few articles
chosen at random, and what prices will your policy entail
when it is in full swing ? You may add one-fifth to their
present cost.

Who has not, during the last pinched years, cut down his
wants ? What tradesman has not stood grimly at his counter,
waiting for customers too poor to come ? If bread, and meat,
and sugar cost us more, do you suppose we can spend gallantly
and gaily as of old on hats and coats and boots ? We shall
not, because we shall not be able. Only the poor, and the
man with an income fixed to a penny, know how hard it is to

buy, even when things are cheap. And so the hardware maker, though he may rejoice over a higher price for his scissors, will bewail a niggardly demand at home. He has kept out things "made in Germany"; but the foreign tariffs are raised, and he exports no more. Little joy is there in selling knives at a rise of 10 per cent. when he sells 30 per cent. less of them.

And what will you say to the hosts of merchants and tradesmen whose chief stock-in-trade is foreign manufactures? And to the entrepôt merchant who imports only to export? How many millions' worth of foreign goods are sent here, to be sent out again every year to every part of the world? Are all these millions to disappear, all these merchants to be bankrupt? And if that is so, what of the clerks they pay, the packers, the messengers, the men who make the cases, the men who import and sell the wood, the shippers who carry the wood, the builders who build the ships? You raise a very inferno of Jack-built houses.

What will be London's fate? I notice that it does not receive at your hands the attention and concern which you lavish on Luton, and yet have you ever considered the vastness of the commerce which comes and goes through the Port of London? London is the clearing-house of the world. From her docks and wharves are distributed from every country to every country the riches of the globe. In one year our London exports and imports were £227,000,000—a commerce growing, and each year giving wages to more men. Do you think if you add 25 per cent. to the cost of everything, and by reducing the imports, reduce in the same ratio the exports, that London will be able to employ the dock labourers, stevedores, sailors, engineers, carmen, railway men and clerks, and to feed the thousands of women and children who depend on these men's wages for their daily food? If you put a tax on food you take from them the little security they now possess. If you put a tax on imports you reduce the volume of trade and throw out of employment one quarter at least of the 700,000 workmen in the great London trades. You reduce the work done by the 250,000 men who are engaged in the transport, the 100,000 clerks, and the 200,000 shopkeepers and dealers. Here, then, are over 1,000,000 persons, the greater number of whom will certainly lose some of their employment by restricted trade, and on each unit of this 1,000,000 depend at least three other persons, 3,000,000 people, the majority of them the weakest and the poorest, all suffering in order that more profits may go to the powerful few.

You doubtless believe that a tariff will bring you more revenue for the military and naval and civil wants of the Government. As I have pointed out, it will only bring revenue by costing the consumer three times as much as the Treasury gains. And have you considered that by this very tariff you are enormously increasing the cost of every Government department? The cost of building ships will be raised 20 per cent., the cost of keeping an army will be raised 10 per cent. Our navy and army will cost us £5,000,000 more a year. Every local and municipal need must be met by higher expenditure, and the rates and taxes which burden us now will be increased by one-fifth.

To all, then, but to a few favourites of fortune or of ministers, Protection will deal a heavy blow. The endeavour to keep an article at one definite price is certain to end in failure. A thousand things vary the cost and raise or depress the demand. There is no finality in tariff legislation, because it is the legislation either of ignorance or of corruption. Thus protective tariffs are vexatious in their incidence and effects. Imposed by officials who, with the best will in the world, have no practical knowledge of the industry they tax, they often succeed in strangling the trade they seek to protect. The trader is for ever met by new conditions—by rises and reductions, reductions and rises. His customers are as much at sea as he is—not knowing from day to day what price they must pay for their goods, with little faith in the present, and no security for the future. Little wonder that such burdens give method and justification to concealment and fraud.

Let not the employer forget that a rise in the cost of food, ensuring a decreased consumption, will lower the efficiency of the workman. What awaits him, burdened by a heavy rise in the cost of all his materials? He cannot charge more for his finished goods without reducing the demand for them. He will then, as does the German, lower the wages of his men and lengthen their hours of work. The men will get, perhaps, more employment, as you promise, but is this the kind of increase which they will relish?

To the man with a small and fixed income Protection is an evil with no mitigation. The workman in an industry which enjoys high Protection may perhaps claim and receive a rise of wage, but how will fare the clerks, the half-pay officers, the vicars, the curates, the Government officials, the widows, the pensioners, the annuitants? * Who will give to them a margin of income to meet the new demands on their scanty purses? How will the clerk with his £150 a year, on which he now lives in pathetic self-denial, be able to meet the higher cost of living for which £200 may not be enough? You will force the poor widow with her £100 a year to pinch and starve to make it do the duty of £130.

For the workman Protection holds no charm against the dearth of employment. The successful Protectionist is the most fickle and volatile of masters, now pouring forth wages with extravagant hand, and now withdrawing every gift and leaving his men to starve. The gambling and the fever which the tariff breeds is the destruction of equable and regular work. The truth is that no nostrum or any fiscal system will secure unbroken employment for the workmen. Depression comes in time to every trade in every country, and the iron workers in the United States suffer as much as the confectioners of Great Britain.

---

* Your contention that the consumer does not pay the duty is a pleasant theory based on air. The consumer always pays the tax either wholly or in part, or more generally with an addition. I have shown how the Frenchman, the German, and the Italian pay their corn duties and something more. If the duty makes no difference, why are a pound of Colman's Mustard, a packet of Epps's Cocoa, a pot of Keiller's Marmalade, a tin of Huntley & Palmer's Biscuits, priced (allowing for freight charges) 30 per cent. higher in New York than in London? Or compare the prices of the same articles imported from a foreign country into England and America. You buy a pound of macaroni in London for 3d., and New York for 5d., cloves cost 1s. 10d. and 2s. 11d. respectively, sago, 2d. and 3d. And if you ask for a tremendous proof of the way in which Protection raises the general cost of living, here is one. You can buy in London things made in America cheaper than you can buy them in New York. That is, in spite of the cost of packing, freight, and insurance, the conditions of life in Protectionist America are so onerous that her citizens have to pay more for the salmon which they tin than a Free Trade Englishman pays for the same salmon in Oxford Street.

Employment must decrease. You cannot reduce imports, most of which are materials for making something else, without reducing not only exports but also home-selling goods. You cannot reduce our home and foreign trade without throwing out of work thousands of our workmen. Excepting in a few industries, which are strong enough to force their claims on the Government and to gain an almost prohibitive Protection, the wages of the workmen will not rise, and as the cost of living must be raised by at least 20 per cent., it follows that the wages of most of the poor will be reduced by 20 per cent. For we must ever remember that a real wage is not a piece of money, but the quantity of bread and meat and house room which this money will buy. If therefore all these things cost more, and the man's wages remain as they were, as the cost rises so does he earn less.

The workman then suffers in every way. He has to work longer hours for less pay; he becomes the slave of powerful and merciless monopolies; and his daily food, which is his chief item of expenditure, is wickedly and out of all proportion enhanced in price. The man with £20,000 a year will spend one-twentieth of it on food and feel little of the tariff in his food bill; the workman who spends 60 per cent. or more of his wages on food is pinched by the smallest rise in cost.

And now let me close this letter by placing before you a human document. It is the budget record from the last Blue Book of a man who lives in or near a town and has a fixed wage or salary.

AVERAGE WEEKLY COST AND QUANTITY OF CERTAIN ARTICLES OF FOOD CONSUMED BY URBAN WORKMEN'S FAMILIES IN 1904.

Limits of Weekly Income	Under 25s.	25s. and under 30s.	30s. and under 35s.
Average weekly family income	21s. 4½d.	26s. 11¼d.	31s. 11¼d.
Average number of children living at home ...	3·1	3·3	3·2

	Cost.					
	s.	*d.*	*s.*	*d.*	*s.*	*d.*
Bread and Flour	3	0½	3	3¾	3	3½
Meat (bought by weight)...	2	8	3	4¾	4	3½
Other meat (including fish)	0	7½	0	8¾	0	10
Bacon	0	6¾	0	9	0	10¼
Eggs	0	5¾	0	8½	0	11
Fresh milk...	0	8	0	11¾	1	3¼
Cheese	0	4¾	0	5½	0	6
Butter	1	2	1	7	1	10¼
Potatoes	0	8¾	0	9¾	0	10½
Vegetables and fruit ...	0	4¾	0	7	0	10
Currants and raisins ...	0	1½	0	1¾	0	2¼
Rice, tapioca, and oatmeal	0	4½	0	5	0	6
Tea...	0	9¼	0	11¼	1	0¾
Coffee and cocoa	0	2	0	3½	0	3½
Sugar	0	8	0	10	0	10¾
Jam, marmalade, treacle, and syrup	0	4¼	0	5¼	0	6
Pickles and condiments ...	0	2	0	2¼	0	3¼
Other items	1	0½	1	3¾	1	6½
Total expenditure on food	14	4¾	17	10¼	20	9¼

Here almost everything but tea and sugar have been condemned by you to taxation, while tea and sugar are already heavily burdened. Observe that another 10 per cent. on the cost will mean to the family a further expenditure of 1*s.* 6*d.* to 2*s.* a week. Add to this the great increase in the cost of rent, clothing, and furniture, and you see that starvation is not very far off.

THE TENTH LETTER

SIR,—No question have you flung more often into the face of the public than this one : If Free Trade is necessary to a nation, how shall we explain the greater prosperity of Germany, France, and America? It is a question very natural and most plausible. But in the first place, it assumes a state of things which does not exist. Prosperous though Germany may be relatively to her past, her prosperity and the comfort of her working classes are not comparable to the wealth and the happiness of our workmen. Nor must you, in making comparisons, forget that no analogy is complete unless the conditions are similar. If you will take France as an example, do not forget that France, Protectionist though she is, is able in most years to grow enough corn for the consumption of her people. The price of bread in those years is seldom high, and the frugal peasant, living on half the wages that suffice to our labourer or artisan, has a lot by no means miserable. But compare the percentage of the unemployed in France and the United Kingdom, and you will find that during the last seven years, while our percentage has been under 4, the French percentage has been over 9. Is this a conclusive proof that Protection gives employment to the protected country? Look at the figures of the French export trade, and you will find that it is stationary, if not declining. And yet France has high Protection. If, again, you wish to understand how an import duty on bread can affect its price, I beg you to see how the wheat duties in France have year by year, and with what you call scientific accuracy, increased the price of the French loaf.

If you prefer to take the case of Germany, here you can be

met on your own ground. It is a country perhaps more
analogous to our own. It has great resources of iron and coal.
It has an agricultural population and great manufacturing
cities. It is, by the tendency of events, paying less attention
to the cultivation of corn and food than to the increase of its
manufactures. But it has certain advantages which we do not
possess. Its population is 50 per cent. greater than our own,
and it should be able, therefore, to turn out a volume of
manufactures far exceeding our own. It has another advantage which we do not possess—a real and ardent passion for
education and technical excellence—and it is the application
of scientific methods to manufactures which has given and is
giving to Germany its rapid advance in international commerce. And yet what do we find? An enormous increase or
Socialism, the direct result of the heavy burden of Protectionist taxation; a body of labourers and artisans badly paid,
badly fed, forced to work like slaves, burdened by high tariffs
on the corn, meat, and necessaries of life which, under a Free
Trade system, would have brought them ease and comfort.
Your praise, too, is inconsistent with your blame, for in one
breath you laud the German tariff and abuse the German
"sweating." If Germany is your Mecca for the workers, why
should her citizens flee from their holy city to a poor and
decaying Britain?

If you will consider an interesting parallel to the present
position of our finances and of the cure which you advise us to
apply to them, let me refer you to the debate which took
place in the German Reichstag on December 9th, 1904. The
burden of military extravagance is becoming intolerable, and
the leaders of the manufacturing and agricultural classes had
formerly advised an increase in the tariffs in order to avoid a
deficit on the Budget. The public is assured that if the tariffs
were increased no greater burden of taxation will fall upon
the poorer classes. The increase in the tariff is allowed. But
see what follows. The leader of the Clerical party, eager
before to show that the increase in the duties would be paid
by the foreigner, is now obliged to admit that the unhappy
consumer {pays the whole increase. The limits of tolerable
taxation have been reached, and the Government are forced
to propose a loan to meet the deficit. "I cannot conceal from
you that the prospect is a very dismal one." Such is the

confession of the German Minister of Finance. Can you listen to it without a tremor?

The commercial progress of the United States, like that of Germany, is due to many causes. Her activity is constitutional and climatic: speed and efficiency are natural to her sons. Her vast spaces and her population give her a world to herself. With an area of 3,000,000 square miles and a population of 80,000,000, it would be strange indeed if she could not produce a greater bulk of manufactures than a country with half the population and one-twenty-fifth of the area. How shall two small islands, with a soil impoverished by the outgoings of many centuries, rival a country nearly as large as Europe, where the rich and virgin earth yields a hundred-fold to the husbandman? How shall not a population of 40,000,000 be closely pursued by 80,000,000? How shall not a giant nation, rich with all the gifts of bountiful Nature, with all the raw materials of manufactures in her own earth at her own door, devoted to trade with a zeal which most men reserve for religion, young, restless, unburdened by the feudalism of Europe—how shall not such a nation press hard, nay, overtake the little island that gave her birth?

And yet with all her advantages, see how she loads herself with burdens almost intolerable. She who, if she were wise, would possess the greatest merchant fleet of the world, sees her materials so enhanced in cost by the selfish greed of her manufacturers that her ships dwindle in number year by year, and that every article which Protection can protect is at famine prices. The Old Man of the Sea is on her neck, and only a miracle will shake him off. That miracle will come when the food supplies of America no longer suffice for her people. Imagine the condition of the American workman when America cannot produce all the food she needs, or manufacture all the goods which are necessary for life and comfort. Imagine the taxes on imported food, now dormant, made effective. Imagine the sudden rise of price, the misery, the panic. In sober truth, America is prosperous not because of Protection, but in spite of it. Give her Free Trade, remove the shackles of the Tariff, and in a few years you will see a mighty giant loosed from his chains, a miracle of commerce.

We have an admirable object lesson in our own great

Colony of Australia. There are two Colonies side by side, with equal opportunities and equal privileges. One was a Free Trade Colony, and the other a Protectionist Colony. New South Wales, the Free Trader, increased in thirty years its population by nearly 300,000, while in the same period of time the population of Protectionist Victoria decreased by 10,000, a movement which proves that the higher wages of the Free Trade Colony were more attractive than the lower wages of her Protectionist rival. The annual trade of New South Wales was £24,000,000, while the whole turnover of Victoria was £18,000,000. Now mark what follows. At the Federation of Australia New South Wales was forced to give up her Free Trade system, and wages now are either stationary or have decreased, while the prices of every necessary of life have increased enormously. See this comparison :—

	Under Free Trade, 1899.				Under Protection, 1904.		
	s.	d.			s.	d.	
Bacon ...	0	8	per lb.	...	0	9	per lb.
Beef ...	0	3	„	...	0	4	„
Butter ...	0	9	„	...	0	10	„
Cheese ...	0	6	„	...	0	8	„
Eggs ...	1	0	per doz.	...	1	6	per doz.
Flour ...	10	3	per 100 lb.	...	13	0	per 100 lb.

And why choose the States and Germany as your cardinal examples ? If Protection is good for nations, surely you are willing to see what it has done for Russia. She stands at the very head of tariff-makers with no rival near her throne. Here duties average 130 per cent. *ad valorem* on manufactures. Here, therefore, you have the ideal state. And what a working model she presents to us, with her starving millions, her crippled industries, her foul corruptions ! Or take Italy, with her 13s. 1d. per quarter duty on wheat, and her impoverished consumers paying the wheat duty and something beyond it, and look at Italy's poverty and crime. Or Spain, with her tariff which reduced her trade by 20 per cent. as soon as it was adopted. Or France, with all her frugality, where the heavy hand of her tariffs makes her trade languish and grow stagnant. Do you speak of British decadence, when a great Protectionist country has gained only £16,000,000 in exports in twenty years ? And if you wish for the finest flower of Protection, go to Venezuela, the Paradise of Tariffs, where, oh happy state and happy citizens! the exports every year exceed the imports in splendid disproportion.

If we are to compare our own progress with the progress of the Protectionists, in simple honesty we must not choose two out of twenty and dismiss the eighteen failures as irrelevant. We must take account of the essential factors of each case. You must not compare a country which can produce all it needs for food and raw material with a country which must import three-fourths of its necessaries. Two men can turn out more than one man, and if you compare the output of two nations, you must tell your audience it *is* two against one. The really great thing is that this little island can hold its own against its giant competitors. Will you compare the producing power of a country of 80,000,000 with the producing power of a nation of 40,000,000?

Nor, above all, must you forget that progress is relative, not absolute. To say that Germany and America are advancing with greater rapidity than we are is to say something which is correct, and yet grossly misleading and fallacious. Shall I call for an analogy from private trade? I offer the parallel case of two traders. If A, who commenced his successful business six years ago, is now making steady, but in comparison with his first years slow, progress, he is, if he is sensible, satisfied. His yearly increase is at all events an increase on a large turnover. Would you not accuse him of unreason and absurdity if he were aghast because the equally able B, starting three years ago, doubled his small turnover in the third year, while he in his sixth year has only advanced by one-eleventh? Look at these figures. They form a simple but an effective lesson in relative progress :—

Year.				Turnover of A.	Turnover of B.
1	...	...	...	10,000	—
2	...	...	...	15,000	—
3	...	...	...	30,000	—
4	...	...	...	45,000	10,000
5	...	...	...	55,000	15,000
6	...	...	...	60,000	30,000

In other words, a moderate increase on a large sum is as satisfactory as a great increase on a small sum, and when the business of B has reached the years of A, his yearly increase will no doubt be reduced to the same moderate proportions. Apply this to Germany and the States, and add also the material consideration that they surpass us in population by 50 per cent. and 100 per cent., and your fears will vanish. To bewail the growth of German and American prosperity is to bewail the growth of their numbers—a lamentation futile and undignified. No mop of Dame Partington will stem the tide of their progress, and unless you can enlarge the area of your country and double her population, you must be content to see the processes of Nature producing their inevitable results. As you said in 1896 :—

"There is no reason whatever for putting forward alarmist views of our position, which are greedily accepted abroad, and which lead our foreign friends and competitors to take altogether an erroneous view of the commercial power and the commercial influence of Great Britain."

And even if under Protection America has flourished, what reason is there that we should flourish with a like commercial policy ? America is a Republic. Do you ask us to become Republican ? It is of no avail to bid us turn our eyes to foreign examples. We are not German, we are not American, neither are we French or Spanish. We are English ; we have won our freedom through much tribulation, and we refuse to leave it for the poisonous atmosphere or the foul growths of Protection. Be comforted. Our wealth is greater than the wealth of any other nation. Our foreign investments are vast and growing each year, and man for man we are far richer than Germany or America. Nor is living so hard to us as to their citizens. Their cost of living leaves little margin for luxuries or saving. To provide his family's food, clothing, housing, coal, lighting and taxes an Englishman has to spend the earnings of 205 days, while the happy citizens of your Edens must spend thus :—

United States	...	...	...	225 days.
France	...	...	...	231 „
Germany	...	...	...	240 „
Russia	...	...	...	286 „
Italy	...	...	...	290 „

I acknowledge that your jealousy of other countries is a natural one. The prosperity of our neighbours not seldom leaves with us an unfavourable impression, it makes us restless and a little discontented. Jealousy, the strongest of our bad qualities, whispers that there is a quality, a distinction, a something which we do not possess. But we need not despair ; our own qualities excite the same emotions in the minds of those whom we envy. It is all very unreasonable and very human.

But do you really hold that the prosperity of one nation is the ruin of another ? It is a poor and dismal creed. Is it not rather true that the growing wealth of our neighbours will enrich us too, and that in the free exchange of commerce we shall, supplying them with things which they desire, and taking from them the things which we desire, reap the reward of that enlightenment which it is your ambition to make dark?

THE ELEVENTH LETTER

SIR,—You may wonder why I have said so little about the " Imperial " side of Protection, why I have kept Colonial Preference to the last. I will tell you. I have done this, to be quite frank, for two reasons. First, because I do not regard Preferences seriously ; secondly, because I suspect that you are doubtful. It is a scheme full of airy nothings—unpractical, impossible and absurd. Already it is dying, your praises of it are perfunctory, your references more slight. As an Imperial mask for pure Protection it was useful ; it has served its purpose and it will go. Whatever your first ambitions, you are now a Protectionist, pure and simple, and as for your followers, they have never been anything else. With what augural smiles do your fellow-Commissioners greet one another when Colonial Preferences are the order of the day ?

I do not question the sincerity of the small band of amiable but uninstructed enthusiasts who tell us that the Empire can be kept together only by 10 per cent.—and believe it. They are the Rump of your once great Imperial party—a little group of hazy fanatics whom all respect and whose wisdom no one trusts. It is because I honour these men that I ask your patience while I consider your Colonial scheme.

It is simplicity itself. You will put a duty on imports and relax it in favour of Colonial imports. Thus American corn will be taxed at 2s. or more probably at 10s. a quarter, while Colonial corn will come in free ; American knives and German iron will bear a 10 per cent. duty, while Canadian iron and cutlery will take their place, untaxed, in the affections of the British consumer. The Colonists, grateful for this boon, will relax or annul their own Protective duties in favour of the

Mother Country. Thus Britain and her Colonies, united in
fiscal bonds, will self-sufficiently defy the world.

Now, before I point out the very obvious difficulties which
beset your path and will make your way impossible, let me
repeat what I have said before ; 80 per cent. of our import
trade and 60 per cent. of our export trade is done with foreign
countries, and more than two-thirds of our food and raw
materials come from the foreigner. You will see at once the
gravity of this statement. It means that we are asked to risk,
nay, to sacrifice our existence as a great commercial nation in
order that our Colonists, who do not need our help, may
become a little richer. Sacrifice there must be, though on this
your attitude is obscure. In your Imperial mood you confess
that we shall lose by giving the Colonies a Preference ; in your
later and commercial mood the sacrifice has passed away, and
only the material gain is present to your view. But it is clear
that if there is no sacrifice for the Briton, there is no gain for
the Colonist. In that case what has your policy to commend
itself to our children across the seas ?

There are three things which make your policy impossible.
In the first place, you have nothing to show that the Colonies
are willing to let our goods in free if we, placing a duty on
foreign imports, allow their imports to enter England untaxed.
Obviously, if the Colonies will not make such an agreement,
if they still insist on laying duties on our imports, there is
nothing "reciprocal" in the arrangement, and the whole
scheme collapses. You say there is an "offer," but the most
careful and microscopic search has been unable to discover it.
When we ask the Government to produce the "offer," Mr.
Lyttelton, your successor, is obliged to confess that no offer
has been made, a statement repeated with equal emphasis by
the late Prime Minister of the Australian Commonwealth.
You, however, disregarding the confession of the Colonial
Secretary, repeat with insistence that the offer has been made,
and you refer us to the willingness of several of the Colonies to
allow us a preference in their markets. This is not convincing.
What we want to see is the offer of something definite from the
Colonies for which Great Britain may be willing to "pay"
(the word is yours). You have told us that the Colonies are
willing to give us "equal measure in return." If that were
true, it would undoubtedly be something, though perhaps not

of the value which you conceive it to be. If you will guide us to the passage in which any responsible Colonial Minister has promised to give us that equal measure, no Englishman will be churlish enough to refuse to consider the offer. But it cannot be found, because it has never been made nor will it ever be made. The simple truth is (and you know it as well as any one) that there is not the slightest chance that the Colonies will allow English manufactures to enter freely in competition with their own young industries. The Canadian Government has told us plainly that their manufacturers will oppose any further Preference in favour of British goods.* What, indeed, have they to gain? First you must settle whether your tariff will raise prices or not. If it does not, obviously there is no gain for the Colonist. If it does, the most they can gain is about 4s. a head. Is it tempting enough?

Nor would the highly practical suggestion of New Zealand compensate us for the millions we should lose by reducing our foreign imports. Mr. Seddon proposes that the old duties on British goods shall remain, but that the duties on the foreigner shall be raised still higher. Such a "Preference" would be worth less than nothing, as you have yourself acknowledged. For did you not point out at the Colonial Conference of 1902, that the experiment of a Canadian Preference in favour of our goods had had no substantial results? In spite of this Preference you showed that the increase of British trade was only 48 per cent., while the increase of foreign trade, taxed by the higher duties, was 69 per cent. Nothing can prove more clearly that it is impossible by Tariffs or Preferences to alter the direction of trade. As you said, unless we can send our goods free into the Colonies, it is no satisfaction to know that other nations are taxed higher than we are. And do you not see how illogical your demand will seem to Canada and Australia? For if free imports are fatal to British goods, how will you persuade Colonial manufacturers that the importation of free British goods into the Colonial market is not equally

* "The Canadian Government has been attacked by Canadian manufacturers on the ground that the Preference is seriously interfering with their trade. The woollen manufacturers have been foremost in the attack, and they have made very bitter complaints to the effect that the industry is threatened with ruin through the severe competition from Britain brought about by the operation of the Preference."

D

hurtful to them? Unless, therefore, you can induce the Colonies to remove their duties on British goods your scheme is doomed, and as you know that they will not remove these duties, you may surely acknowledge that it is dead. But because there are still a few sincere men who accept the possibility of a Colonial Preference, I will not end my letter here

It will not be out of place to quote here (and to do little more than quote) your really remarkable invitation to the Colonies for the avoidance of manufacturing rivalry :—

"But we will say, after all, there are many things which you do not now make, many things for which we have a great capacity for production. Leave them to us, as you have left them hitherto; do not increase your tariff walls against us ; pull them down where they are unnecessary to the success of this policy to which you are committed. Let us, in exchange with you, have your productions in all these numberless industries which have not yet been erected."

I will say nothing concerning this jewel of common sense * save that it sheds a brilliant light on your practical wisdom and your knowledge of man that you should solemnly ask our very practical and energetic Colonists to bind themselves for all time to make nothing which the British make. This by the way.

A second insuperable obstacle is that, if you are to give the Colonies a Preference, you must tax both food and raw materials. You allow that food must be taxed, but you still shrink from a tax on raw materials. Sir, you must come to it. How otherwise will you avoid a flagrant partiality which may well bring about the dismemberment of the Empire? By your duty on foreign wheat you will keep Canada faithful, but how are you going to retain the errant affections of Australia? You will then have to tax foreign imports and to let in her imports free. If you help Australia and forget New Zealand, you will have the formidable Mr. Seddon at your throat. Down goes a duty on foreign mutton that New Zealand mutton may come in free. But, look, South Africa assails you with bitter reproaches. You are losing her loyalty because you refuse to put a duty on foreign wool. It is done, and so you go on from duty to duty

* Afterwards relegated to darkness in the official edition of your speeches.

until there is not a thing, necessary or unnecessary, on which you do not lay a tax.

I shall, in my letter on Retaliation, deal with another formidable danger which awaits your Preferences—the danger of losing the tremendous advantage which we possess under the " most-favoured-nation " agreement. If you favour the Colonies against foreign Powers, this agreement falls, and our traders lose millions.

I have in a former letter asked you how you will reconcile the British farmer and manufacturer to Colonial competition? You tell us that foreign competition is wicked and ruinous, and in the same breath you prophesy the splendid growth of Colonial energy and output. Our Colonies will, under your protecting hand, soon build vast factories and lay down endless acres in wheat. Then will come something of which you do not dream, or, perhaps, to which you ingeniously are blind. The seas will be full of Colonial ships, bringing free Colonial corn and manufactures to force down the price of British wheat and British goods. Can you not hear the cries of British farmers and manfacturers as they accuse you of their ruin? They have voted for you because you promised them relief from the foreigner, and now they demand Protection from the Colonies. How will you resist their plea, and if you cannot, how will you, without a Preference, keep the Colonies faithful? Here I present to you a noble and a patriotic prospect, endless years of friction and jars and jealousies, bitter reproaches—a mother and her sons in savage and sordid strife.

In the third place, you have India in your way? You have spoken much of Canada, of New Zealand, of the West Indies, but of the brightest jewel in our crown, of the country which is the wonder and the envy of the world, teeming with countless millions—of this you say not a single word. You know that our trade with British India is worth £32,000,000, and that this figure more than doubles our total trade with Canada and New Zealand conjoined? Are we to neglect a Possession under our absolute sway, holding a population of 300,000,000, with whom we do a trade which is more than a quarter of our trade with the whole of the British Empire?

Your Preferential scheme receives no support from the Government of India. In an official minute they call attention to the slow building up of their financial stability, their rising credit, and their expanding trade. They urge that it is the free exchange of exports and imports which has made the wealth of India ; and they point out that in a war of tariffs and retaliation, the danger to India of reprisals by protected nations is so grave that there can be no justification for embarking on a policy which may be disastrous in the extreme. Lord Curzon had not before him when he signed that minute an example of the reprisals which he feared. Your Sugar Convention, which prohibits the import of Russian sugar, and which drew from Russia an instant reprisal on Indian tea, presents the Viceroy with an object lesson.

If Protection is necessary for our great nation, and for our established industries, how shall we deny that Protection to the infant industries of India ? Look at the imports of India and you will see that their value is £70,000,000, and that of the manufactures imported by far the greater part comes from Britain. Your theory of trade forces you to believe that every manufactured article imported into a country displaces labour in that country. The cotton manufacturers in India have long agreed with you, and time and again have urged their Government to impose a heavy duty on the cotton goods which we send them every year to the value of over £20,000,000. The answer of the British Government has been clear and obvious. The benefits of Free Trade have been proved by the experience of fifty years, and in compelling India to be a Free Trade country we are conferring on her the benefits which our own people enjoy. Can you now, by any decent excuse, refuse to India the benefits of that policy which you praise, which, indeed, you are determined to enforce upon Great Britain ? And if you do grant their claim, how will you bear the laments of a ruined Lancashire ? For of our industries the cotton industry is one of the greatest, and of our cotton goods one-third are exported to India, and pass into her ports free of all duty.

These then are three hindrances which you cannot put away. Your whole ambition, indeed, is founded on a quick-sand. The ideal of a federated Empire is a noble and, it may be, a possible one : the ideal of a self-sufficing Empire is vain. And even if it were not vain, you could only find your basis of fiscal union in absolute Free Trade within the Empire. But

the British Empire is not homogeneous.   You cannot compare
it to America or Germany.   It holds a hundred peoples with a
hundred varying wants and ambitions.   To force these contrary
elements into one mould is impossible.   You would produce
discord out of a false harmony.   You would do a thing fatal to
the very essence of our Colonial polity.   We lean on freedom,
on complete independence for Mother Country as for children,
and to replace the love and respect which these sustain by
a 10 per cent. Preference is surely a mean close to a noble
history.   The relations of trade do not beget affection : restricted by tariffs, they can only induce jealousy and friction.
It is useless to tell us that we suspect and condemn that which
we do not know.   Colonial Preferences are an old tale.   France
has tried them, Holland in the East Indies and Germany in
her Colonies have sought in vain for success along the lines of
your policy.   We made the experiment in years long past, and
we gave it up in despair and disgust.   The same failure will meet
a new attempt, and the failure will be the more dangerous,
because the vast and innumerable interests at stake are ten
times greater than they were a century ago.

THE TWELFTH LETTER

OF RETALIATION

SIR,—To the mild Protectionist the word Retaliation has a soothing cadence. It seems to whisper of manliness, of justice. It has all the vigour of Protection without its vulgarity. It is therefore in great request and popularity with that large class which would have the *soupçon* of the hog without its coarseness.

Now the essence of Retaliation is that you should be able to strike effectively. To retaliate by tariffs and duties on another nation you must be able to make your blows felt. Otherwise you will beat the air in a ridiculous and costly way. I understand that the three branches of your policy are—(1) to keep the Empire together by Preferences ; (2) to protect our Home industries and to increase our wealth ; (3) to punish the foreigner for his insolent duties on our manufactures. In other words, you will impose duties on foreign goods to force them to remove the duties which they lay on our goods.

Have you considered the enormous difficulties which beset Retaliation as they beset Colonial Preference ? Against whom will you retaliate ? Clearly against those powers which inflict on us the heaviest burdens. Here then is a list of the Protective nations in the order of their tariffs. It is an instructive table :—

Estimated average *ad valorem* equivalent of the Import Duties levied by the under-mentioned Foreign Countries and British Possessions on the principal Manufactures exported from the United Kingdom :—

	Per cent.
Russia	131
Spain	76
United States	73

						Per Cent.
Portugal	...	...	...	...	...	71
Austria-Hungary		...	...	...	...	35
France ...	...	...	...	...	...	34
Argentine Republic	...	...	...	...	...	28
Italy	...	...	...	...	...	27
Germany	...	...	...	...	...	25
Sweden ...	...	...	...	...	...	23
Greece ...	...	...	...	...	...	19
Denmark	...	...	...	...	...	18
Canada (Preferential Tariff)	...		...	...	...	17
Roumania	...	...	...	...	...	14
Belgium	...	...	...	...	...	13
Norway ...	...	...	...	...	...	12
New Zealand	...	...	...	...	...	9
Japan	...	...	...	...	...	9
Turkey ...	...	...	...	...	...	8
Switzerland	...	...	...	...	...	7
Australia	...	...	...	...	...	6
South African Customs Union (Preferential Tariff)	...	...	...	...	...	6
China ...	...	...	...	...	...	5
Holland ...	...	...	...	...	...	3
British India	...	...	...	...	...	3

You must obviously begin your operations by attacking America, Spain, and Russia ; and you must, if your blows are to be felt, lay your duties on the goods which they send us in greatest volume. You will therefore lay a duty on the cotton and the wheat of the United States, on the iron ore of Spain, on the wheat of Russia. And remember that unless the blow be heavy it is of no avail. Your duty must be heavy. If you are fighting a nation which lays a 50 per cent. duty on our manufactures, it will be absurd to fight her with a 5 per cent. or a 10 per cent. duty. You must take your courage in your hands and place 25 per cent. on her imports.

This sounds possible and even easy. But what would be the result of a duty of 25 per cent. on foreign corn and iron? Are you prepared to increase the price of the loaf by one quarter? If so, you must be prepared for a revolution. What, again, will you do if the other country is not impressed by your fisticuffs, and if, hardening its heart and budging not one inch, it increases its duties on our manufactures? You will have then to retaliate by higher duties ; and will you, for an indefinite time, risk an increasing burden on our trade, while you lay an intolerable load on the poor ? Do you not see that of all nations we, the greatest manufacturers of the world, are the most vulnerable ? that for every blow which we can deal the foreigner, he can deal us three, and each one heavier than our own ?

But assume that you are successful, that after a tariff war of years, during which our commerce has been disorganized, thousands of traders ruined, and a hundred millions lost, you have forced the other nation to reduce her burdens on our goods. Elated and triumphant, you remove your taxes on the foreign imports, when lo! from every quarter of Britain and her Colonies savage cries and threats break upon you ; your own citizens accuse you of their ruin ; the Colonists menace you with imperial dismemberment. Do not you understand what you have done? Intent on your tariff war, you have not seen that, secure from foreign rivalry, weak and unhealthy industries have been building new factories and engaging new workmen ; you have forgotten that the Colonists, enjoying their Preferences while foreign goods are shut out, have developed new trades and borrowed more capital. If you remove your duties on the foreigner, the home trades cry, "Can we stand against a new rush of imports ? How will fare our industries, and whither go our capital?" And from the Colonists comes a sterner reproach. "You have told your countrymen," they say, "that without Preferences the Empire will be shattered into fragments. If you remove your duties, our Preference ceases, and the doom foretold by you comes to pass."

I have spoken before of the arrangement which we called "the most-favoured-nation" treatment. By that agreement we have secured from every nation this most admirable and profitable condition, that in every case where a Power lowers its tariff in favour of another nation, British goods shall enter the ports of that Power on the lowest duties which it imposes. If, then, France shall lower its duty on a Russian import from the higher tariff of 30 per cent. to 15 per cent., British goods at once and automatically enjoy the reduced tariff. But—and mark this—if we, through Retaliation or Preference, make an exceptional arrangement with a Power which the other Powers do not enjoy, we are removed forthwith from all the privileges of "the most-favoured-nation." Who shall say how many millions of pounds you will sink into the fathomless abyss, how many traders you will ruin, if in your reckless haste you expose us to the heavy hand of the foreign retaliator?

Have you never read the stories of these tariff wars in which you urge us now to become combatants? What struggle will you hold out to us as a fair model for success of all the sad and stupid quarrels into which avaricious and savage traders have forced their unhappy countries? All for greed and spite, State after State has seen its commerce wounded almost to death, its trades struck down, its people robbed of their bread. And was the final victory so great? There was no final victory. The nations, ashamed, exhausted, and impoverished, have always sunk to the miserable peace of desolation.

Read this story of ruin and waste. In 1888 the French and Italian Governments entered upon a war of Retaliation. Heavy duties were established on Italian imports. Italy replied by heavier ones. The war lasted in its acute stage for two years, and smouldered for three years more. The results of the struggle to the commerce of the two countries it is impossible to express in figures, but we know that the French exports to Italy fell from £13,000,000 to £5,000,000, and that the Italian exports to France fell from £12,000,000 to £5,000,000 ; that France, which had before taken from Italy nearly 3,000,000 hectolitres of wine, in 1888 took only 17,000. The exports of silk from Italy to France fell from 28,000 quintals to 7,000. The French exports of woollen goods fell from 20,000,000 frs. to 6,000,000, frs., and every other article of commerce of the two nations suffered in similar proportion. Who gained by the struggle? Not Italy, not France. The competitors of the two countries looked on with delight, and reaped their reward in the trade which France and Italy flung away.

The story of the French tariff war with Switzerland has similar features. It commenced with the usual threats, and it ended with the usual exhaustion. It lasted for two years and six months, and it meant for Switzerland a reduction in its exports to France of nearly 40 per cent., and a reduction of

French exports to Switzerland of over 40 per cent. Again the rivals of the two countries reaped the reward. Three results ever follow a tariff war—the trade between the combatants is not recovered for many years; if it is recovered at all, each combatant loses fifty times as much as she gains; and the wiser countries gather up the business which the unwise ones might have enjoyed. Of all quarrels, the quarrels of commerce are the most savage and deadly. For money makes men cruel. You tell us of Germany. Has she been able by Retaliation to lower the Dingley duties on any manufactured article. Has France, with her "big revolver," fared any better? You would willingly answer "Yes," but facts and recent history are too strong.

Do you ask us, who have not known for fifty years the methods of these sordid battles, who have remained in our tents safe and untouched, while our neighbours slay each other, to lower ourselves to the level of these miserable and ineffectual bludgeonings?

THE THIRTEENTH LETTER

SIR,—You have yourself supplied Free Traders with their most deadly weapon. You have given us an object lesson, a working model of Protection which we cannot forget, because its results face us at every turn. The Sugar Convention of 1902, into which, as Mr. Walter Long says, the Government entered "largely at the instance of Mr. Chamberlain," is well known to you, nor can you have forgotten the points of the Convention, and the arguments by which you induced the House of Commons to sanction it. You remember the position of things before the Convention. The sugar refiners in continental countries received bounties or gifts from their several Governments for the encouragement of export sugar. If foreign sugar could be sold at £10 a ton in England, and if the foreign Government gave its sugar merchants £4 a ton on every ton sold in England, the foreign seller would be able to sell his sugar in England at £6 a ton, and still make his profit. Hence followed this most admirable result, that by the folly of the foreign bounties we bought our sugar at a price so low that great industries were founded on sugar and flourished exceedingly, that we were able, not only to supply the home market with cheap jam, biscuits, confectionery, and mineral waters, but to export these goods at a low price, and to undersell the foreign manufacturers in the very countries in which the sugar was produced. You will note that, as usual, the miserable consumer in the foreign countries was obliged to pay considerably more per ton for his sugar than the price at which it was sold in England. There were only two drawbacks to this most comfortable state of affairs. The foreign sugar, chiefly beet sugar, sold at so low a price, forced down the price of the cane sugar from our own West Indian Colonies, and the same cause brought about a depression in the sugar refineries of the United Kingdom. But compared with the enormous boon of cheap sugar, these drawbacks were of little importance.

Here you have an excellent example of the misguided policy by which a foreign Protectionist Government, artificially fostering an export trade, fine their own citizens to the abundant satisfaction of the Free Trade consumer in the other country. It came to pass that the foreign Governments grew tired of their generosity to the British public, and were willing to agree that sugar on which a bounty had been paid should be forbidden to enter this country. Had such a suggestion been made twenty years ago, it is not difficult to imagine the indignation and scorn with which you would have received it. But things are not as they were. The West India planters and the English sugar refiners called loudly upon you for Protection. Their social and parliamentary influence was great, and sugar has always been able, with wheat, to command attention to its woes. They pointed out to you the melancholy position of their industries, and they asked you whether you would consent to allow British Colonies and British merchants to be struck down by the dumping of the foreigner. And so, although it was proved by irrefutable evidence, that the Sugar Convention would not benefit the West Indies to the extent of more than £250,000 a year, that the sugar refineries employed an inconsiderable number of men, and that for the sake of these two small interests it was ludicrous, and more than ludicrous, to punish a whole nation, still, in your new-born ardour for Protection, you fell into the pit which was being digged before your very eyes. The Government agreed to keep out all bounty-fed sugar, including enormous supplies from Russia and Argentina, the two countries which refused to enter into the Convention. What is the result? Russia has retaliated by placing a heavy duty on Indian teas, and we have wounded our own dependency. Cheap sugar is no more. This raw material, which is the basis of the great industries of jam, biscuits, confectionery, and mineral waters, and which is one of the prime necessaries of life both to rich and poor, has increased in price by nearly 80 per cent.

It is impossible to evade plain facts and dates. There has, for many years, been on the average a distinct downward tendency in price—now checked. The duty on sugar was imposed in 1901, and at the end of that year sugar was 8s. 9¼d. per cwt. In 1902, although the supply had increased, the price rose to 9s. 1½d; in 1903, with a further increase in the supply, the price rose to 10s. 1d.; while in another year, with a small decrease in the supply, the price has risen to 15s. 4½d.

The chief blot and the chief act of folly is to prevent the importation of those supplies from Russia and Argentina. Put into definite figures, this means that the British public is now paying for sugar £8,000,000 more than it paid before the Convention, while the increased profits of the West Indies, which appear to be sending us less sugar than ever, and of the sugar refiner, may be reckoned at not more than £500,000 a year. The great sugar industries are either unable to purchase their sugar at the prices now ruling, or they cannot sell their goods at the higher prices which the increased cost of their material enforces.

No more convincing proof of the fatal folly of Protection, Preference, and Retaliation can be found than in the facts disclosed at a special committee meeting of the Confectionery Section of the London Chamber of Commerce on December 21st, 1904. It is clear that not only the great confectionery trades, but that the enormous mineral-water trade are suffering acutely from your policy. The former, which before the Convention employed 100,000 workers, has been obliged to dismiss 12,000 of them, and to place 50,000 on short time. Its profits, which were rising before, are rapidly disappearing, and the immediate future is under a thick and melancholy cloud. In the mineral-water trade the prospect is one of equal gloom. An enormous amount of capital has been invested in this trade, which has been rapidly increasing during the last ten years. The fatal folly which prevents the importation of sugar from Russia and Argentina has forced up the price of all sugar. It has favoured, as Protection always favours, the corner and the monopolist. The signature of the Convention has thus resulted in an immediate increase in the cost of sugar, a necessary and the most costly factor in the manufacture of mineral waters. With a rising cost and a decrease in the demand, this trade is becoming demoralized. A great firm with a capital of a million, making before the Convention an annual profit of £70,000, is now making under £20,000. Another firm, making in the past £25,000, now has to confess to a loss of £2,000 a year. And remember that these are the great and wealthy houses. Of the 3,500 mineral-water manufacturers, a great number must be trading on a small capital, and, unless an effort is made to assist them, they will disappear with their workmen into ruin.

Nor should we pass by the thousands of large and small traders, grocers, confectioners, and general shopkeepers, the main prop of whose business must be sugar-made -goods. They see before them the same ghastly future. The food caterer is no less heavily burdened. There are 6,000 cheap caterers in London alone, all doing useful work in providing cheap and wholesome food for the working man. What does it mean for them? It means ruin to many, a struggle to the rest. The rise in the price of sugar will apparently soon be 100 per cent., and the increased cost of a penny cup of tea or cocoa must either be borne by the caterer, or he must charge the customer $1\frac{1}{2}d$., an increase which will reduce the demand enormously.

Another and a natural result follows. Sugar bounties being at an end, the price of sugar in foreign countries is enormously lowered, and the consumption has enormously advanced. The Continent gains by our folly, and its increased consumption amounted last year to 889,000 tons. New confectionery businesses are springing up to take advantage of the unwonted cheapness of sugar, and it will not be long before they export their goods to Great Britain to undersell our already half-ruined industries. The fact that a "corner" has been possible in sugar may be to some extent an explanation of the rise in price, but it is an obvious condemnation of your methods. Protection is the parent of trusts, and you have given us a foretaste of what will come upon us when all our imports are subject to your policy.

Here, then, is your working model. It has the three features upon which you have set your affection. It Protects the West Indies and the sugar refiners from "unfair" competition; it is an example of Retaliation and of Colonial Preference. We have used Lord Lansdowne's revolver with which to threaten Russia and Argentina, but in our clumsy hands the revolver has only wounded its user. Notice, too, another thing. All your prophecies, all your assurances, have collapsed. You told us that by this Convention every one would be pleased, every one satisfied, and that no person except the foreigner would suffer. Mr. Balfour, with dramatic emphasis, assured the House of Commons not only that no increase in the price of sugar would result but that in all probability the price would fall far lower. Better far to have voted the West Indies a subsidy of half a million a year than to prop up their decaying trade and unprogressive planters at the cost of £8,000,000 a year to our population. We have placed our interests and the existence of one of our great industries in the hands of a committee of foreigners. We have thrown away our own advantages, and have handed them over to our rivals. We are debarred from importing sugar from two great sugar-producing countries. We are making an annual loss of £8,000,000 in order to benefit the West Indies by a quarter of a million. And this is practical politics : this is the triumph of a business man.

THE FOURTEENTH LETTER

SIR,—Protectionists are of two classes. The first class desires Protection because it desires higher prices for its goods. The second desires Protection because its leaders praise it, because it seems bound up with the Imperial theory, but chiefly because of want of thought. The first class I can hardly hope to persuade, though some may be wise enough to see that a ruined England is no market for their goods. In the second there are many to whom settled conviction has not yet come. The attitude of such men is one of the paradoxes of life. The average business man is cautious and conservative to the point of timidity. Advise him to reconstitute his own affairs on a foreign model, and he will rightly answer that what is good for another man need not be good for him. Alas! he hears your trumpet voice, and away fly his prudence and his common sense. But sometimes they come back, and so it is for him that I ask your permission to give in simple terms the main outlines of the Free Trade theory.

The essence of a Free Trade tariff is that a duty shall be imposed only for revenue and not to protect an industry. Every pound paid by the consumer thus goes into the Treasury, and not into the pockets of the protected manufacturers. The vice of the Protective duty is that it raises the price of the home-made article in an almost equal degree, and the consumer pays a double duty. For every pound that goes into the Treasury three pounds go into the purse of the manufacturer. Again, high tariffs reduce imports, but to reduce duties is to increase revenue.

Free Trade is the triumph of simplicity over complication ; of bold wisdom over timid and selfish prejudice. Its essence is uniformity—uniformity in the treatment of all commerce, home, Colonial, and foreign. The defenders of Free Trade base their tenets on facts and results, not on à *priori* axioms and vague generalities. The Protectionist may produce plausible theories and exceptions, but the Free Trader, while he may allow their abstract excellence, will tell you that the results at which they aim can only be attained by costly and uncertain methods, and that Free Trade does in general reach the same ends by cheaper and simpler ways. Protection must raise the price of the things protected, that is its *raison-d'être;* but though Protection may increase the profits of a particular industry, it increases them at an enormous loss to the community through national waste. It draws labour and capital from their natural channels into channels more difficult and costly, and it thereby reduces the annual produce of a nation.

The obligations of international trade are mutual, and if we confer a favour on another nation by receiving her food, she confers another on us by buying our manufactures. Each produces what it can produce most cheaply and efficiently. Moreover, it is clear that if we reduce the other nation's imports we reduce our own exports. For it is only by exports that we can pay for imports, as it is only by his imports that the foreigner can pay us for our exports. Protection must, therefore, to a greater or less extent limit our markets, reduce our output, check invention and energy by removing competition and new ideas, by placing the wealth of the country in the hands of a few, instead of distributing it among millions. Freedom of trade, on the other hand, enlarges markets and exports, cheapens the necessaries of life by ensuring a healthy competition, increases the efficiency of the manufacturer and the workman, encourages development, and makes the whole nation wealthy and contented. The Free Trader does not deny that under Protection some nations may flourish ; but he says that in such a case unusual conditions will be found, and that they are the exceptions ; that, as a rule, Protection impoverishes a nation, and that a Protectionist nation flourishes in spite of, and not because of, its tariff.

Finally, he asserts that any attempt to cure by Protection the evils of which the Protectionist complains will but double the loss. " That insidious and crafty animal, vulgarly called a statesman or politician," will, if he attempts to direct the affairs of business people, quickly display his awkwardness and ignorance ; he will expose himself to the corrupt demands of interested traders, and, though he may sincerely oppose these demands, he will yield to them. Before either he or the people is aware of it, he will have fastened on the people's back a load heavy and irremovable. This is an imperfect world, and well-meaning persons will always be trying to redress balances. But in the long run, interference with the methods of free exchange will tend to make the balances more disproportionate, and will play into the hands of the shrewd and the selfish.

No man was born a Free Trader any more than he was born virtuous. The carnal man is a monopolist and a fighter. It is only by prayer and fasting that the evil spirit is cast out, and that a man sees facts without the distortion of prejudice. When he does see them, you will have some trouble to blind him again. The practical man does not start with theories, he starts from the observation of facts. He sees things occurring in more or less regular sequence, and if he is intelligent, he begins to found on this sequence certain laws. These laws will not be scientific, because the man is not highly trained, but they will be none the less useful, and when he is asked to believe that they are not based on facts he will require very clear evidence of their faultiness. He worships no monster of perfection, he obeys no fiscal decalogue. But he has heard what Protection brought in days gone by, he knows what Protection brings abroad. He will have none of it.

THE FIFTEENTH LETTER

SIR,—I am now approaching the close of my task, and I doubt not you will be abundantly grateful. It has been necessary to speak faithfully, and you will do me the justice to say that I have attempted to touch, however superficially, on most of the facts, figures, and arguments which you have laid before us. I have described your policy, and have proved to you how great are its dangers, both to our imperial and financial well-being. I have shown how all your readings of history are incorrect ; how your figures are unsound, your facts wrenched from their context and set to grotesque uses. Is it strange that the arguments based on such perversity have failed to convince a common-sense people ?

It is not true that the lower classes were happy and well fed before the abolition of the Corn Laws: they were miserable and half-starved. It is not true that our trade is stagnant : our trade advances by sure and steady steps. It is not true that our great industries have been ruined by Free Trade : in spite of your condemnation they flourish. Every sign points to abounding and increasing wealth and comfort. The enormous fall in the price of food, the distribution of wealth among all classes, the rise in wages, the reduction in pauperism, the decrease in crime, the balances at the savings' banks, the growth of our foreign investments, the vast volume of our shipping, the progress of our imports—all these are proofs, strong and stable, that Free Trade has made us rich. It has made us something else. It has made us an honest people and has given us an honest Parliament.

You have seen how the imposition of a duty on one

article ensures a demand for Protection all round, and I have shown how the first and modest demand of the Protectionist grows monstrous until the ability of the public to pay becomes the only limit of a duty. I have. shown how Protection takes from the consumer a far greater sum than it pays into the Treasury, how a moderate tax on corn would, by raising the price not only of foreign corn but of colonial and home corn also, rob the consumer of £15,000,000 and only benefit the Treasury by £5,000,000. Nor will you fail to notice that the more Protective your duties are, the less goods will be imported and the less money will flow into our national coffers, until a final and prohibitive tax will stop the entry of a single penny.

I have shown that if you are to give a preference to the Colonies, you cannot use Retaliation by a moderate tariff. For as soon as by Retaliation you conquer your rival, you must remove your tariff; and how without a tariff can you "prefer"? Your only remedy will be to impose a flagrant tariff, and to bargain with the foreigner by offering to take off 10 per cent. In that case, what price will our food be? Retaliation, indeed, is the most insane of policies. As Mr. Gladstone very concisely said, the Protectionist maxim is this: *If the foreigner strikes thee on one cheek, strike thyself on the other.*

I have shown how Protection impoverishes the general for the benefit of the few. Placing barriers in the way of free exchange and a natural division of labour, it creates an inequitable division of wealth. It causes enormous waste, and lessens the wealth of a nation. The riches of 100 rich Protectionists may exceed the riches of 100 rich Free Traders, but the aggregate wealth of a Protectionist population is far below the wealth of a Free Trade population of equal size. We have seen how Protection favours the powerful industries against the weaker ones, how, artificially raising the prices of commodities, it inflicts on the small trades, as well as on the whole people, an intolerable wrong. As you yourself once said, "Any proposal to tax corn is a proposal to put rent into the pockets of landlords, and any proposal to tax manufactures is a proposal to put profits into the pockets of particular favoured manufacturers."

The only foundation of stable government and progress is the material well-being of the masses. It is useless to say that this is a sordid view of human affairs. Affairs *are* human, and the public interest can only be regulated by the homely common sense which governs the private citizen. Economy is as necessary to the state as to the individual. Profuseness in expenditure, though it may have an outward glory and magnificence, though it may attract the idle and the parasite, weakens the moral fibre and makes a state impotent when the lean years come. National wealth is not sought as an end in itself, but because it alone, by giving national power, makes possible the progress and the self-respect which save a nation from revolution or decay.

And now what shall we say for your policy? First prove to us its necessity. If we were falling back, if we were declining as a commercial nation, I could understand your concern, though I could not approve your cure. But we are more prosperous than ever. Faults we may have, but decadent and decaying we are not. Old we may be by the standard of our rivals' age, but by the years of the world we are young indeed. Who shall say that we are even now approaching the healthy middle age of a nation?

In truth you, the Imperialist, are committing an act of the grossest treachery. You are belittling England and maiming her resources. Who will rejoice so much at your success as our rivals? It is against Free Trade, because they hate and fear it, that the other nations have built their tariff walls so high and strong, and it is only by Free Trade that we have conquered and can conquer. Our cheap exports, made cheap by untaxed materials and untaxed food, pass over the steepest wall, but how shall they enter if we are burdened by your heavy imposts? If a cheap export hardly prevails, how will a dear one fare? We sell our goods to the Colonies as to the foreigner because we are the cheapest sellers in the world, and we are the cheapest sellers because our food is cheap and our materials cheap. It is by Free Trade that we undersell our rivals in their own country; if we tax our imports, and raise the cost of everything, how shall we pour our cheap manufactures on a foreign market? The foreigner will smile, for where will be our export trade?

If you give us Protection, you must give us more magistrates. Industrious as our judges may be, they will not be able to cope with the crime which Protection brings. Cheap food and good wages give Innocence its chance; dear food and low wages are the parents of Crime. Little need of proof for this. All men know and feel it; but, if you will have a proof, you have only to read how, since our heavy taxation for South Africa and our dearer bread, crime and pauperism grow and the prisons are fuller. An empty stomach knows no law. How many preventive men will you endow to watch the hordes of smugglers whom your tariffs will create?

If you wish to place against your morbid imaginings the outlook of a healthy mind, read these words. They are the words of Mr. Reid, the Prime Minister of Australia :—

"When the day arrives that England can only maintain her trade by artificial preferential tariffs, on that day England is doomed. A time may arrive when England must place tariffs around herself, but they will be the very last ditch on which a defeated nation attempts to defend herself against conquering foes. England gained her supreme commercial position, not by barricading her ports, but by proving herself superior in technical skill, in manufacturing utility, in knowledge, in business habits. She must ultimately rely on these weapons for her success if she is to retain her high commercial position. Technical education, improved methods of production, the study of foreign requirements, the adaptation of goods, are the weapons with which England must fight if she is to hold her own."

Admit the claims of weak industries for Protection, and there is no limit to the demands which will assail you. Every decaying trade, working on some exploded fashion with feeble energy and old machinery, will become eloquent over its dismissed workmen and its lost capital. Will you have the moral courage to refuse these petitions? If you have, do you suppose that your Parliamentary supporters will be able to defend themselves against the threats and bribes of men who have no scruple? You say you will only protect the industries which can show just reason for complaint. But how will you test their fitness, save by the votes which they can command? Protection grows by what it feeds upon. The landlord and the manufacturer assure the public that they will never ask for more. But Protection raises the price of everything. They will quickly find that 2s. on wheat and 10 per cent. on manufactures do not compensate them for the increase in their

expenses, and that they are as poor as they were before.
Another turn is given to the screw, and the 2s. becomes 5s.,
and the 10 per cent. grows into 20 per cent.

The Protectionist politician is the bond-slave of every
interest. He dare refuse no claim, he dare resist no bribe.
To every industry he must offer relief: his note-book
is full of genial promises. Does he go to Greenock? then
sugar shall be raised. Is Rochester calling? then cement
shall be protected. Do the Lincoln farmers complain? a tax
on wheat is imminent. Is Wales among the grumblers? tin
plates shall soar to gold. Is St. Helen's decaying? our
mirrors shall cost us double. Does Liverpool abhor the cheap
watch? we shall change two sovereigns for our Waterbury.
Is cheap glass an abomination to you? then huzza for the
2s. tumbler. Does faithful Birmingham demand the right-
ing of the wrong? then pearl buttons shall be as dear as
diamonds.

Behind your movement, and using you as their tool, are rich
manufacturers and foreign financiers. The former hope to
secure a monopoly for their goods at the cost of every class ;
the others know that they will have a noble field for the
exercise of their financial genius. You say that your satellites
are framing a tariff for the Empire's glory, and not for private
gain; that the consumer shall not suffer. But why do these
men sit round the table of your Tariff Commission? Why are
they elaborately framing duties on foreign imports of the
goods they make? Do you tell us they are actuated by
unselfish aims? If Protection is not to increase the price of
their goods, why are they there?

You are bringing the canker of Washington to West-
minster. In America political corruption is supreme. The
election of a Senator is the open auction of a seat. The
millionaires buy not only legislators, but legislatures. The
whole atmosphere reeks with corruption. You will find
the lobbies full of traders, imploring, threatening, bribing,
corrupting. The gorge of an honest man rises at the sight.

Dissociate private profit from political duty. Political corruption is a blow at the heart of a nation. Let Protection
come, and the purity of our institutions, the reputation of our
lawgivers, is gone. We are only human, and the corruption
which has made Parliamentary Government a reproach and a

rottenness in America will soon make an end of our honesty. With your lobbyings and your bribings, your "influences" and your "adjustments," your trusts and your monopolies, your checks and your counter-checks, your drawbacks and your rebates, the festering growth of tariff corruption will soon hold our senators in thrall. There is only one free Parliament in the world, and are you bent on binding it in chains? For monopoly kills honesty and liberty, and if we lose Free Trade we lose our freedom. No nation is free which is at the mercy of its industries.

Your imperial aims are ill directed, for the policy of a self-sufficing Empire is impossible, and why should we desire a national exclusiveness? Half our greatness and all our culture have come from foreign stocks, and we can no more stay the play of international forces than we can stop the flow of the rivers. To refuse to admit the inventions and the wares, the literature and the arts of other nations, is to condemn ourselves to hopeless stagnation—social, intellectual, and commercial.

You set the Mother Country against her Colonies: you bring discord into the empire. The price of wheat has fallen, and the consumption of wheat has risen. You know, for a quarter of a century ago you told the House of Commons, that for each fall of 2s. a bushel in the price of wheat the death-rate falls 3 per cent. Are you willing to see our people dying faster that our Colonies may be bribed to loyalty? Will you enter the cottage with its intolerable rent, will you argue with the workman with his low wages, will you gently speak to the wife and children with half a loaf and no meat and little sugar—telling them that they must sacrifice something for a lofty idea, for Empire, and for Colonies which need no sacrifices of the poor?

The Colonies are bound to us by the indissoluble bonds of affection and self-interest. They are our sons, and without our aid their independence is at the mercy of any Power. Their love comes from the common history of a common stock; from the freedom which mother and children alike enjoy. Do not think that they will join with our enemies. They will not, and if they would, you will not make them more loving by 5 per cent. Men are tiring of your Colonial heroics, of your unceasing talk of Empire. They are beginning to ask

where England stands in your heart, whether in your
grandiose visions your eyes have failed to see the little island
with so much to give and so little to receive. A cry will arise
of " England for the English." You are begetting a host of
Little Englanders.

You have many on your side, I know, whose minds are
swayed by no corrupt motive. Honest but unwise they are.
These men mistake empty bustle for the regular and patient
methods of common sense. Their theories are bubbles,
mere figments of sentiment and rashness, which fall to
pieces at a touch. The whole policy, indeed, is marked by
the trivial omniscience of the amateur. A group of men,
half of them without political instinct and half without
business capacity, are busy making an imperial and glittering
toy. Little flags are planted here and there : here and there
regions are enclosed by barbed entanglements. *Here only
the Empire shall trade,—no foreigner shall enter here. You, my
Colonial friends, shall deal only with such and such: we will deal
only with such and such. We will make so and so ; you will make
so and so : we shall lose so much ; we shall gain so much. Our
income will be this : your income will be that. See how beautifully
the whole complicated scheme works : how the myriad wheels revolve
in infinite play : how the mechanism shall obey the mandates of our
will.* Poor doomed machine ; alas ! the first blast of an
untoward wind will make you wreckage—your foolish wheels
all whirring and broken, while your makers weep and chatter
round your ruin.

It is war and domination that have set you on the search
for war's sinews. The war of the Imperialist, with its vast
call for money, is the opportunity of the Protectionist.
It was after the Civil War that the industries of the
United States called for assistance. It was after the war of
1870 that the French trades demanded monopoly. It is
after the war in South Africa that British traders are using
patriotism as the mask of greed. The real secret and the true
causa causans of Protection is Imperialism. The Imperialist
is jealous of the foreigner, ambitious of a self-sufficient Britain,
timid of progressive rivals. He does not see that the prosperity of another country is a new means of wealth to us ;
he sees only a definite amount of business for the nations
to scramble for. His aim is to reserve the good things of the

world for the British, to shut out the things made in foreign lands, to develop in Britain alone the means of our support, to keep the rest of the world in economic barbarism.

On this Imperialism (a spurious Imperialism at the best, and at the worst a degraded hypocrisy) Protection in the economic sense has in these latter days based its demand. The landlord or the manufacturer, anxious to raise the price of his land or wares, plays upon the Imperial chord, and by appealing to the patriotic instincts of his countrymen, he wins the support of many who, without such a motive would see the fatal folly of the scheme. It is this combination of patriotism and finance which is so unspeakably loathsome. There are two hypocrisies, the one of religion, the other of patriotism. In the name of both have great crimes been committed, and behind both have rogues taken refuge. But the meanest things have always been done by the shady Patriot.

In truth, the trail of the company promoter is over it all. The magniloquent prospectus, the bombast of Empire, the third-rate heroics, the cheap quotations, the fluent fallacies, the promise of unutterable profits, the inspired paragraph, the chatter of the journalist, the needy peers, and behind, but unseen, the thievish men who work the puppets. How well we know it all, the men who chant with alien lips the praises of England, the imperial finance, the solemn congratulations, the forcible but dignified rebuke of the suspicious, the patriotism and the cash! No wonder that the rich man takes up his thousand and the poor man his ten shares; for who would not merge the grossness of money-getting in the fervour of the missionary? There is also the excitement of many tongues, the beating of many drums, the spending of the money, the betrayal of hopes, falling shares and failing confidence, the plausible excuse, the easy promise of a better day, and at last, the collapse of the burst balloon. How ignoble it all is, how old, how stale? How often did our ancestors hear the same gross and material appeals, the same greedy patriotism? Have you ever reflected that if Free Trade is a musty shibboleth, Protection is an antediluvian curiosity?

You cannot by new terms alter the qualities of things. Protection is robbery whatever you may call it.

> In vain we call our notions fudge,
>   And bend our conscience to our dealing,
> The Ten Commandments will not budge,
>   And stealing will continue stealing.

Do not ask us to re-write our whole history, to erase the laws of common sense. Character is the foundation of Empire, and character overleaps boundaries. We are a little land, and yet we lead the world. It is by our character that we have won our place, and not by the policy of the parrot and the monkey.

We are menaced by a conspiracy as dangerous as any Stuart Cabal—the conspiracy of the unscrupulous rich. A gang of wealthy and clever rogues—born, in part, of alien stock— have by their flattery made you their tool. What do they know of England ? What love have they for England who cannot speak her language or think her thoughts or dream her dreams : whose only aim and only hope is to pile up their mountainous gold out of her bowels ? And it is for these men, that they may form their corners and their trusts, their combines and their monopolies, that you ask us to surrender the freedom of our trade, the honour of our Parliament, the liberty of our press. Sir, we will not do it. We know them now. It is for them that you have impoverished the whole land with your war and your taxes ; it is for them that 20,000 of our soldiers have left their bones in South Africa. You offer us dear bread and cheap Chinese. We refuse your gift.

Whatever be your faults, you are of our stock : you are English. Are you not weary of your subservience to foreign wiles ? Come away : come forth from their reeking tents into the fresh and open air. Forbid them to lay sacrilegious hands on the vast and delicate fabric of our commerce, raised by the energy and foresight and wisdom of great Englishmen. Stable and strong it is, but if you set a thousand interests pulling at its structure it will fall. Forbid them and come away.

THE LAST LETTER

OF YOURSELF

SIR,—You will, I doubt not, agree that the economy of states and of individuals should be based on the same principles and proceed from the same motives ; that the common sense and elevated selfishness which govern the lives of successful men should find their counterpart in the rulers of states. But, in the intercourse of nations, we have forces which disturb and dislocate the even progress of affairs—prejudice, jealousy, blind hatred, and ignorance. Thus you will find that a man who in his private career has always followed the guidance of prudence and politeness, will, in the conduct of political and international affairs, display a folly, an obstinacy, and an obtuseness of vision which in his business concerns would have made him bankrupt in a year.

Why is it that the world is governed with so little wisdom? It is because the rulers of men refuse, or are not allowed, to display in politics the qualities which make a man successful in private life. Why, Sir, has your career, so brilliant and vigorous, so full of meteoric flights and dazzling flashing changes, been so empty of practical result ? I would fain do you no injustice, for you have great qualities of heart and mind. I do not couple you with the men who flatter you for their own evil purposes ! Into what strange company have you fallen ! You, who once were the colleague of Gladstone and Bright and Salisbury and Devonshire—now the consort and the leader of fourth-rate politicians, of doubtful economists, of foreign financiers. You are nobler than they, and yet how shall I praise you?

I do not impugn your motives. You have shown in many fields the ardent devotion of the warrior for his cause. But I do impugn your wisdom. The end is one but the ways are many, and it is no excuse for rashness that it seeks a goal by paths that will never reach it. Be impetuous if you will, be bold, be dashing, but let your impetuosity, your boldness, your dash, come from the mind that sees the end and can command the means. Sentiment is a good ally but a poor master.

Unstable as water, tossed about by every new doctrine, the profligate and libertine of politics, you have ruined the two parties of the State. Soldier of fortune, you have known the fierce joy of conflict under every flag. Firm to no anchor, everything by turns and nothing long, irresistibly driven from pole to pole, the mouthpiece of other men's ideas and interests, you have passed through the whole gamut of experience. The champion of Home Rule and its bitterest foe, the author of Majuba and the destroyer of the Boers, the Jack Cade of Lord Salisbury and the idol of his nephew, the hero of Free Trade and the prophet of Protection, Little Englander and Imperialist : each contrary creed inspires in you an equal passion ; each varying fashion you defend with the same lucidity. To you causes are but counters, words but baits, figures but illustrations. Nothing has a separate meaning. To you the opposite of a creed is as the creed itself. What does it matter if to-day two and two make six, where yesterday they made five, or last year four ? What does it matter if yesterday you held the Tories in hatred and to-day you hold them in love, that yesterday you asserted what to-day you contradict ? Nothing really is, really matters, except that you must lead, must crush, must overcome. *I* only am, *I* only matter. For *me*, for *me* the earth turns, the planets whirl. That is the one thing which is real, that will bring all jarring elements into union and peace, that can justify all contradictions, absurdities, errors, falsehoods, treasons.

What have you done for England ? What home is happier for your years of power, whose career is one long procession of broken pledges? Most unpractical of men! Have you ever contributed an original measure to the sum of the national welfare? No! yours is the mind that watches the tendency of things, the ebb and flow of events. Vigilant and keen, you ride on the crest of the flowing tide, careless whither it takes you, and so secretly aghast at the results of your own incompetence, enraged at the vanity of your own prophecies, you press onward to new dangers. *After me the deluge.*

Is not your crop of wild oats at last garnered? Will you not even now learn the lessons of prudence? Cease to be the slave of words; cease to offer a cure for every mortal woe. Phrases are not facts, and rhetoric is a poor substitute for truth. Things are what they are, and no sorcery will alter their results. By what magical arts will you make every one richer by making everything dearer?

I admit your patriotism, but others are patriots too. Cease to monopolise the virtues. A sincere man does not carry his heart upon his sleeve; he is reticent about the inner things of which the shallow man prates. The religious man does not vaunt his religion, nor the honourable man his honour, nor the patriotic man his patriotism. He takes it for granted that every man is as religious, as honourable, as patriotic as himself.

The time is short and passes. Learn at last to follow the simple and direct path. Eschew the elaborate futilities and mazy speculations which delight the doctrinaire. Simplicity is the mark of great schemes, great thoughts, great men. Complication comes from timidity, mistrust, subtilty. Wisdom is but a superb common sense. Cease to torture us with your decadent fears! Cease to despair of England!

He that withholdeth the corn, the people shall curse him; but blessing shall be upon the head of him that selleth it. You have been the knight of Free Trade; will you be the champion of monopoly? Will you in your old age hear the curse of the poor, the cry of the widow? Read these words; they need no praise. They are Peel's farewell to the Commons:—

I shall leave a name execrated, I know, by every monopolist who would maintain protection for his own individual benefit. But it may be that I shall leave a name sometimes remembered with expressions of goodwill in the abodes of those whose lot it is to labour and to earn their daily bread by the sweat of their brow, when they shall recruit their exhausted strength with abundant and untaxed food, the sweeter because it is no longer leavened by a sense of injustice.

Do you despise this noble hope ? Let not your epitaph be,

HE MADE BREAD DEAR.

LaVergne, TN USA
24 October 2010
202031LV00004B/105/A